WAYS OF THE
WILDERNESS

WAYS OF THE WILDERNESS

A Personal Journey Through Religion and Literature

Anne McPherson

NOVALIS

© 2003 Novalis, Saint Paul University, Ottawa, Canada

Cover: Richard Proulx

Cover Painting: Tony Urquhart (*My Garden from the Cave*)

Layout: Christiane Lemire, Richard Proulx

Business Office:
Novalis
49 Front Street East, 2nd Floor
Toronto, Ontario, Canada
M5E 1B3
Phone: 1-877-702-7773 or (416) 363-3303
Fax: 1-877-702-7775 or (416) 363-9409
E-mail: cservice@novalis.ca
www.novalis.ca

National Library of Canada Cataloguing in Publication

McPherson, Anne
    Ways of the wilderness : a personal journey through religion and
literature / Anne McPherson.

Includes bibliographical references.
    ISBN 2-89507-405-4

    1. Wilderness areas in literature. 2. Wilderness (Theology).

I. Title.

PN49.M36 2003   809'.9332   C2003-904090-9

Printed in Canada.

We acknowledge the financial support of the Government of Canada through the Book Publishing Industry Development Program (BPIDP) for our publishing activities.

5   4   3   2   1   07   06   05   04   03

For D.R.K. and B.F.M.

in memoriam

— ACKNOWLEDGMENTS —

This book is dedicated to the late David Kinsley and the late Ben Meyer, who supported and enlightened me during my research into the symbol of the wilderness at McMaster University. Once, during a particularly bad patch, when I was becoming discouraged, Ben said, "Why don't you give up this academic study of the wilderness and just write your book?" Twenty years later, here it is.

My warmest thanks go to Ian Shaw and John Porter, who read the manuscript as it progressed, and offered generous and helpful comments and suggestions.

My great appreciation goes to the editorial staff at Novalis: to Kevin Burns, for his enthusiasm and pursuit of the project; to Anne Louise Mahoney, for carefully piloting the work into finished form; and to Derek Bianchi Melchin, for his scrupulous and sensitive copy editing.

— CONTENTS —

Introduction

— THE ANCESTRAL WILDERNESS —

Literature is conscious mythology: as society develops, its mythical stories become structural principles of story-telling, its mythical concepts, sun-gods and the like, become habits of metaphorical thought.

Northrop Frye, *The Bush Garden*

...I don't chide you for wanting to go into the wilderness. I am sure more people will have to want to go and get there before things will get better....

Flannery O'Connor, to Dr. T.R. Spivey, 18 July 1959

...these poore wormes...

Edward Johnson, *Wonder-Working Providence of Sions Saviour in New England (1654)*

I think that, if you go back far enough, all our ancestors had to confront a wilderness before they could establish a habitation, whether permanent or nomadic.

At the very beginning, so one myth of origins goes, our common ancestors left their bounteous, cultivated garden for an unknown place beyond it that had never been touched by human hands. I can imagine what bleak chaos it must have been, since the animals were originally all in the garden too, and the trees, the flora, and so forth. No biblical writer took the trouble to describe what this extraparadisiacal terrain looked like. All we know is that domesticating it would require hard, never-ending work. Perspiration is the first bodily function awarded to men by God after the fall. (Women were given childbearing pains.)

When I think about the long trek from prehistory to our own personal histories, I realize that our forebears must at some time or another have had to repeat Adam's and Eve's experiences. For some of us whose families came from the Old Country to the New World, it's even possible to trace the exact moment when the original settlers began to make their homesteads on the still unsown land.

In the spring of 1635 the Reverend Peter Bulkeley, with his wife and children, left England aboard the *Susan and Ellen* for New England. On 12 September he and another minister, John Jones, bringing with them about 60 others, founded the first inland town in the Massachusetts Bay Colony and called it Concord. I am the tenth generation after Peter Bulkeley, and if I were looking for one source of my longtime interest in the wilderness, I would start right here.

His surname appears in early documents as Bulkeley, Bulkly, Buckley and even Buckly, but I shall call him Peter, even though his portrait makes him seem formidable enough to make one hesitate at such intimacy. My mother and grandfather always referred to him as "Peter," with a fondness that made me think when I was young that he lived not too far away and might drop in at any time. Peter was the only remote ancestor on any side that they ever mentioned; as for the rest of the family tree, it could well have been chopped up for firewood and kept in the cellar.

Peter, like his father, was a graduate and later on a Fellow of St. John's College, Cambridge. Both were ordained, and Peter inherited from his father the rectory of Odell, Bedfordshire, and a handsome fortune. Preaching seems to have been his strength, as he was made a university preacher at Cambridge in 1610. Later, however, he sided with the reformers of the established church, who were termed Puritans, and in the 1630s ran afoul of the new Archbishop of Canterbury, Thomas Laud, who had promised the king he would stamp out heretical views. Peter was "silenced," told he might not preach, teach or celebrate communion—in other words, he was fired. Many clergy in his situation hid out with friends for a time, preaching surreptitiously. Most eventually fled England for the continent or the new world.

(Ten years after a gagged Peter Bulkeley left England, Archbishop Laud was imprisoned by the Cromwellian party and executed, just as his king was to be beheaded four years later. In the matter of ecclesiastical propriety, ruthlessness was emblazoned on both sides.)

These first "planters" (they "planted a colony") came to the new world to preserve their liberty and perhaps their lives. Their main purpose in coming there was much more high-minded, however. They saw before them a "desart wildernesse" in which they would found a new commonwealth of covenanting members. They would become a city on the hill, a new Jerusalem, a light for the world. Their New England was to be a model for Old England, their freedom here allowing them to show the way. They were a biblical people, a new Exodus tribe, bound by what they called a covenant of grace, what Peter Bulkeley called the Gospel-Covenant. By their establishment of a commonwealth, and by their exemplary lives, others would notice, take heart, and copy them.

So the wilderness before them was both a danger and a possibility. Many of these civilized ex-pats (one family out of forty had members with a university education) had never chopped down a tree, never sown a field, never driven off a wolf, and certainly never confronted a wilderness inhabitant. The Indians from whom the Bulkeley contingent bought a six-mile-square of land were of great help to them in planting their first crops. Still, some contemporary writers called them "brutish men," "fierce and barbarous." It was a risky, stern, and difficult life at first in this "howling desart."

What is it about Peter Bulkeley that draws me to him? Heaven knows, we must be quite unalike in our views and ways. He was an iconoclastic Puritan, devoted to the Word; I am a small "c" catholic, lover of the most jubilant and beautiful forms of praise. He was self-sacrificing; I am not. He was a rebel so true to his faith that he spent his inheritance helping to build a holy community in the wilderness. I live on a see-saw of skepticism and belief without the courage to jump off and stride away in a fearful new direction.

It must be that Peter is so much of what I am not—not an alter ego, but an alter conscience. He is what I will never be, and would (somewhat) like to be. (I'd never give up the spine-tingling beauty of Monreale or St-Hilaire or Chartres, or the ethereal music at King's College, Cambridge—see how appealing the see-saw is.) His dedication and his courage are what I lack. His giving up of home and native land with all their comforts: he could, after all, have become a gentleman farmer and waited out Laud. His willing endurance of the hardships of building a new settlement in the wilderness. The joys of religious freedom must have been

severely tested by pioneer living. I am too lazy and self-indulgent to at
tempt anything that even lightly resembles that. My wildernesses, such as
they are, are of a different nature, and most of them not of my choosing.

I can remember exactly when and how I first began to think seriously about the wilderness, when it became my "word," as a good friend
tells me it is. Almost 40 years ago I came across a book by H.A. Williams,
then dean of Trinity College, Cambridge, called *The True Wilderness*. The
title came from one of the sermons intended for Lenten digestion Dean
Williams had preached to the students. Lent, he said, is not the time for
doing "a good orthodox grovel to a pseudo-Lord." The true wilderness is
one in which you find yourself alienated from the people and pleasures
you have always loved, when you come to see your taken-for-granted
world as a fiction:

> ...perhaps I've been robbed, robbed of my easy certainties, my
> unthinking convictions, that this is black and that is white, and
> Uncle George was a saint, and what they told me to believe is true
> and the opposite false, and my parents are wonderful people, and
> God's in his heaven and all's right with the world, and science is the
> answer to everything, and St Paul was a nice man, and there's noth-
> ing like fresh air or reading the Bible for curing depression....[1]

This wilderness experience, says Williams, is part of one's growth,
although when we're in it we're tempted to believe it is all there is, that
the bloom is off the world, there is nothing we can do to help others or
ourselves. Only despair is left. He points out that it is the Spirit of God
who throws Jesus—and us—into the wilderness to be tempted with these
ideas.

Williams' sermon struck me forcefully at a time when many friends
and acquaintances were in great distress and without any means of
alleviating it. I was unhappy that I couldn't help. (I know now that I had
a big investment in the persona of a helping friend, which I didn't seem
to be very good at.) The true wilderness, I realized, was not a place but
a state of being: not just my being, but that of others, of the world, in
fact, some of the time. I was struggling with questions about how to live
my life authentically within the tradition I knew well and loved. There
was lots of introspection, cubic yards of emotional morass, self-
centredness masking as piety, but there was some genuine caring also. I

really was pushing into what I thought were spiritual depths, trying to enter any interior mansion that would open to me.

My wilderness was made up of moods of discouragement; recognition of weaknesses, faults and sins; failed attempts at becoming someone new; asking the age-old questions, more about the hows than the whys of the Christian program and vision—I thought I understood the whys. All the while I was able to surround myself with an exceptional family, stimulating friends and students, music and literature, good conversation, good food, a pleasant house and garden. Yet, despite all these fine ways of being connected to the world around me, I felt much of the time that I was in the wilderness. Clearly it wasn't a wilderness of complete physical, intellectual, or emotional deprivation.

For years this wilderness became part of my picture of the world, and a condition I experienced frequently. I probably connected it with some notion of existential angst, but I didn't try to work this out theologically. The wilderness was, if anything, a symbol, not a disputable idea.

When I was pursuing religious studies at university and searching for a thesis topic that would be close to my personal interests but not so close that I would lose the appropriate "distance" from it, I began to look at the biblical wilderness. I tracked it from its lengthy appearance in Exodus, through the psalms and prophets, into the gospels and apocalyptic literature. To my amazement, although I could see fragments of Harry Williams' and my own notions there, I found so much more. I realized that my symbol was puny in comparison to that of the Hebrews—that their whole history and raison d'être took them back over and over to the great salvation story, in which God led them through the wilderness for 40 years towards the promised land. As time went on, more and more meaning accrued to the wilderness as biblical writers unfolded its many aspects. This mighty symbol captivated me then, as it still does today. As it did my ancestors, too.

The high purpose and holy vision of the "errand into the wilderness" held by the first planters has probably never been equalled since. The Puritans' later excesses and abominations are well known, but by the time of the Salem witch trials the wilderness had been eliminated, and with it the sense of a struggling Exodus community. What had been the Puritan ideal commonwealth slid over into the American Dream. The frontierspeople of the American west attacked the wilderness from different perspectives altogether. They had no intention of being the light of the world. To the north, the people in what was to become Canada, too, pushing their way through the wilderness, looked for the country's wealth of furs, lumber, minerals, to bring prosperity to the struggling new territories. Religious freedom and heaven-bent goals were never taken up in the way the Puritans had espoused them.

Perhaps the overarching metaphor attached to life in the last century has been one of motion. Unlike our nineteenth-century forebears, we are constantly on the move—changing jobs, houses, political and religious platforms, families. The last significant shift in my family's home base occurred when my great-grandmother Hannah Louisa Maria Bulkeley left Fairfield, Connecticut (Peter's third son had gone there as a minister) to marry William Smith, who came from Montreal to establish the telegraph in St. Catharines. They moved into a house on Church Street, where they both eventually died. My grandfather was born in the same house and died there 96 years later. Divorce has been practically unknown in our family. My parents, my grandparents too, regularly cancelled each other's votes, and the only changes in several generations of the family's religious affiliation (except for me) came with marriage—for the sake of the children, it was said. My father ran the business that was started by his grandfather, and although we moved about a great deal when I was young, the moves came as a result of two great external factors: the Depression and World War II.

Today the convictions and the stability of living that kept our ancestors in one place physically and conscientiously have disappeared. Depression and war had far wider-reaching effects than just rearranging the furniture into different spaces. While the directive that took my father to war had a clear and honourable intention—it was a "good war"—it was perhaps the last of the wholly absorbing and understood goals to encompass our society. It brought people together in faith, in fear, in communal love and loyalty.

There are two kinds of perpetual movement that persist today. First is the relentless pursuit of knowledge, notably in science and technology, and of self-satisfaction, with regard to acquiring power and its concomitants. The way towards these goals is not always sure, but it is known. For some, these movements are all-consuming. Second is the type of movement that we engage in more or less consciously. It is directionless, goalless, and tentative. It is not hurried, nor constant, nor regular. There are few guidelines, if any, and the books that have been written to assist us are mostly out of date. Our movement is spurred by the question "Why?" or perhaps "Who am I?" or, as Northrop Frye suggests, "Where is here?" These are questions asked by the well-fed, who have the time for them, and by the unfed, whose cry is desperate, and whose need for an answer is crucial.

The mythic fragment that corresponds so well to this second, life-determining movement is a biblical one, that of wandering in the wilderness. People have been using the phrase to picture their lives ever since John Bunyan began *Pilgrim's Progress* with "As I walk'd through the wilderness of this world...." Bunyan's idea of the wilderness, like that of the New England Puritans—as a place to be endured, in which the struggle to do right is the single proper action—is only one of a complex of meanings held by the biblical wilderness. As the image is transferred from one context to another, from the story of Moses to the prophets of the Exile to the New Testament, many other variations and contradictory meanings appear, but the idea remains essentially the same.

The symbol of the wilderness is rooted deeply in our culture, beginning with the Bible. Old folkloric tales carried it along—stories of pilgrims' hardy ventures, fairy tales of children lost or enchanted. It is a central figure in quest narratives, especially the Arthuriad. Grandly, even before Bunyan, Shakespeare showed us its bleak and cruel aspect in *King Lear*, its terminal state in *Timon of Athens*. As it moved from its originally sacred context to a literary one, it brought with it many of its meanings, and often most of its resonance. New attributes were added, giving an even richer tonality to the symbol. What had been faintly implicit in the biblical symbol was brought clearly into play by writers working in a more consciously literary mode. Most important for us today is its appearance in the work of many twentieth-century authors, such as Atwood, Banks, Beckett, Bellow, Berger, Kennedy, O'Connor, Roth, Roy, Wiebe, Wiesel, and more.

The wilderness, wherever and however it is found, stands hugely against the constraints of our lives today, as imaged by the city, the enclosed garden, the wired world, the dominance of the intellect over the body and spirit, the known, classified and understood, even the written word. Thank God it is endless. But it is not always pleasant or easy to be in.

The wilderness matters because of its negativity, its absences, its freedom and lack of control. It is a source of new vision, new growth, and potentiality. I think it is one of the most significant symbols in Western culture. It is the locus for reintegration of the person, where insights come from, and where they can be collected to form new symbols, ideas, and goals. It is also the place of sorrow and pain, but one pushes through the wilderness in search of new being.

It often emerges primarily as the wilderness of the mind, as in Beckett and O'Connor. It impinges upon us in the West in its geographical magnificence and its terrifying aspects, as in Roy and Wiebe. Some writers—Atwood, Bellow, Frazier, Kennedy—show how interior and exterior wildernesses combine to change the individual, who may be the reader, or the hero, or both. Others show us the nasty urban wildernesses we live in, as do Roth and Berger. They do not all present the whole world as a vale of tears.

In modern fiction we can see the old biblical narrative fragments reappear: the wandering in the wilderness; the scapegoat thrown out into the wilderness; the voice in the wilderness; the holy assembly of the desert; the prophetic cries against the wasted city. We see the same movement through the wilderness as a series of tests, pitfalls, and revelations. We see glimpses of the old promise that the wilderness can be made to bloom again.

Considering Frye's description of literature as conscious mythology, we can understand how the literary and the real worlds connect, the one setting up the other. Which comes first, the present reality or the universal myth? Prescience or justification? Or should one just call it slippage, that wonderfully illuminating movement from the particular to the universal and back again? My way of understanding it is that literature spurs me to look at the present in a new way, giving meaning to what I had taken only to be chaos, or brute data. Sometimes it is the interrelatedness of books with each other and with experience that sets me thinking or noticing or writing, perhaps even to changing my sense of being.

In my previous book, *Walking to the Saints*, I characterized myself as a pilgrim striking out to visit sacred shrines and sites, with plenty of questions and mixed feelings about what these places divulged to me. That is one approach to my life's progress. I certainly knew where I was headed, but not what I would find when I got there. The other approach, also familiar to pilgrims, is formed by innumerable entrances into the wilderness, a place where even the paths are unclear, if paths there be. It is, as you will see, not an easy place or state to describe, because it has so many different facets and sources. A wilderness experience will be different for everyone; it will even change as your life goes on. In my case the wilderness that I thought and wrote about 30 years ago is not the one I know now. All of these occasions of being in the wilderness, or contemplating it, have for me a biblical underpinning. One of the (probably disputable) claims of this book is that the wilderness of the Bible is the source for most Western consciousness of wilderness today. To the extent that my own experience is part of that, I hope that a few personal insertions into the literary show and tell of the book may not go astray.

Whether inspired by ancestor worship and love of biblical symbol or propelled by the question "Where is here?" I think that ultimately I delve into the wilderness for the same reason as Thoreau, another Concord man, did: "We need to witness our own limits transgressed, and some life pasturing freely where we never wander."[2]

1

THE BIBLICAL WILDERNESS

Before it can ever be a repose for the senses, landscape is the work of the mind. Its scenery is built up as much from strata of memory as from layers of rock.

Simon Schama, *Landscape and Memory*

As for you, your dead bodies will fall in this wilderness, and your sons will be nomads in the wilderness for forty years, bearing the weight of your faithlessness, until the last of you lies dead in the desert.

Numbers 14:33

That is why I am going to lure her
and lead her out into the wilderness
and speak to her heart.
I am going to give her back her vineyards,
and make the Valley of Achor a gateway of hope.
There she will respond to me as she did when she was young,
as she did when she came out of the land of Egypt.

Hosea 2:16-17

As soon as I begin to think of the wilderness I come upon a resounding paradox. In its most distinctive aspect the wilderness is seen as the place where experience is unmediated, where you confront yourself and everything else directly—no lies, no beguiling comforts, no disguising screens, only your deepest fears, driving motivations, and clearest intuitions. When you go into the wilderness there is no protective cover.

The paradox is, though, that it is through the complex mediations of myth and literature that we have learned what we know of the wilderness we may now be in. Without story, image, language, there is no wilderness, just as it may not be too far-fetched to say that without speaking of God there is no God to speak to.

Whenever you go into the wilderness, however you may imagine it or visualize it or spend time in it, you do not go naked or empty-minded. You take with you—you cannot help it—the wealth of your own cultural background, or some of it at least. The wilderness is not a void, and neither are you.

Because the wilderness is seen as vast, disordered, deep, and mostly uncharted, one might be tempted to think that it could represent any fearsome or unclassified place, any bewildering situation or loathsome emotional swamp. Although plenty of people use the word loosely, it really doesn't mean just anything at all. Its roots are biblical, its extended branches always connected through metaphor and meaning to its roots. Our Western culture, even though no longer dominated by the Judeo-Christian religious tradition, has absorbed, consciously or unconsciously, the symbols and narrative structures of the Bible. So it is the biblical writers who give us the first great image of the wilderness, a rich legacy from which other thinkers and writers may draw.

I haven't always read the Bible for interest or illumination. As a fairly regular attendant at Sunday school I couldn't escape it, but I can't say that I was persuaded by the snippets we studied to pursue the matter further. As someone said, my religious life survived despite my church school education. Later on, in an attempt to regulate my spiritual life, for many years I read the biblical lessons proposed for daily reading, and the Psalter. These were often inspirational, sources for thoughtful meditation. Just as often they were obscured by my fatigue, or by their content, which was either boring or weird.

I now possess about a dozen Bibles, in various states of repair. Some I have inherited: my Presbyterian forebears all had their own. I have a 1593 "breeches" Bible, so called because it is the only translation in which Adam and Eve are said to have used the fig leaves to sew breeches: all the other versions say less modestly that they made aprons. I have a 25-pound 1854 family Bible, with everyone's vital statistics written in by my great-grandfather Walker and his descendants. In my father's, Jesus' words are printed in red. And there's a little 1868 beauty, with a gilded cover and a gold clasp. Both of these are in the familiar King James translation. On my own I have amassed several contemporary translations; I shall use my favourite, the Jerusalem Bible, throughout this book, because of both its scholarship and its beauty. One is in French. And finally one Hebrew Bible, barely touched—I had such foolish hopes of learning the language.

Just owning interesting versions of a text doesn't make one a devoted reader, however. It took the encouragement of a friend, and the inspiration of a teacher, to get me started. Harry Mansfield, an Anglican priest in Niagara, was the one who pressed me to take those daily biblical readings of middling interest and write down my thoughts about them. "You're always trying to think about something, so why not these?" The practice surely opened up their content in unexplored directions; as to whether my interpretations gave any respect whatever to the original texts, I do not know.

One day in the faculty/graduate lounge in the religion department at McMaster University, where I had enrolled to study the sociology of religion and other matters (but not the Bible), I was having coffee with a group of people, some of them strangers. One of them was excitedly describing a particular problem in biblical scholarship. He spoke beautifully, was so fascinated by the intricacies of the problem, and was besides that such a cheery, engaging person. I was captivated on the spot. After he left I said to a friend, "Who is that? Because whatever he's teaching, I'm taking it." I took three courses from Ben Meyer, a professor in Ancient Near Eastern studies, and loved every one of them. I began only then to peek into the rich composite of *ta biblia*—the books that comprise our sacred texts. There is much, much more to uncover.

The biblical writers are a varied lot. In many cases we don't know who they are; in others, we know that several minds have contributed to the final edition of many of the books we know collectively as the Bible. Some books are flat, unadorned narratives; others are the work of colourful, distinctive personalities. The image of the wilderness turns up everywhere: in songs of praise, dire warnings and diatribes, predictions of the end of the world. First and foremost, though, the writers think back to the main event in Jewish salvation history, the story that is told in the books of Exodus and Numbers, in which God brings his enslaved people out of Egypt through the wilderness into the Promised Land. The story of what happens there—the miraculous events, the leadership of God, the apostasy and repentance of the people—is told by different writers over the centuries, and reinterpreted according to the situation the Hebrews are in at the time.

What happened in the wilderness during the Exodus is such an important occurrence that the wilderness becomes a symbol for subsequent events and heroes. It almost seems as though, if you are going to be a leader (or if you have become wicked enough to deserve God's wrath), you will have to experience the wilderness in one way or another. So it is that, after Moses, the ancient prophets Elijah and Elisha go there. So does John the Baptist; so does Jesus. When the Hebrews of Judah are about to be carried off into exile in Babylon, the prophets Isaiah and Jeremiah compare their wicked behaviour with that of their ancestors in the wilderness. During the Exile, another Isaiah comforts them with visions of a wilderness redeemed and flourishing.

A purely physical description does injustice to the biblical wilderness, because wherever it appears, it does not do so as landscape or background, but as significant ground, and often as inscape. Still, it is important to see how it was first described physically in order to show how the biblical writers are not bound by the look of it. They use the word "wilderness" also to refer to other places and spiritual states that have no visual relationship to the original description, and yet share in the meanings that such a description evokes.

The fullest picture of what the wilderness is like comes from the writings of the prophets—not, as you might expect, from the accounts of the Exodus, which are straightforward narratives lacking description. In the latter we learn a lot about the behaviour of the people after they leave Egypt, but little about their surroundings, until the prophets fill in the description for us. It seems that the more remote the writers are from the main wilderness event, the more significant they find it to be, and so they furnish it with meaningful details relevant to their own present day.

The wilderness has several persistent characteristics wherever it appears. In the first place it is always unsown land, a pasture, a heath, a common or a seasonal desert. The Hebrew word for this is *midbar*. It may have grass or it may not, it may be flat or mountainous, but it is always dry, waste, and hot, except after great rain, which comes seldom. Agriculture would not flourish here because of the uncertainty of rain. Herds can be pastured here at certain times of the year; at other times it is too dry for them. So, the wilderness is not a desert of sand (*arabah* in Hebrew), but an uncultivated tract of land that becomes sterile at certain times of year owing to lack of rainfall. It is uninhabited, except for nomads and their flocks, an abandoned place, which comes to be seen as a place where one can or must be alone, for whatever reason. Those who dwell there temporarily live either in tents or in caves. There are some permanent inhabitants, however: jackals and ostriches, wild donkeys and wolves, lions and leopards and wildcats. Evil spirits have their home there, as do vipers, kites, and that mysterious dark figure of Lilith. In certain situations angels come to the wilderness to give aid.

Food and drink are a problem. Water is not potable. I think of the bitter water the Hebrews found at Marah, which Moses sweetened with God's help (although there are some wells, such as the one with sweet water the slave girl Hagar finds to nourish Ishmael). No food is available: one must provision for one's sojourn in the wilderness, or be provided for by some non-natural means.

The vision of a lonely place inhabited by wild and unusual creatures and spirits already hints at meanings and experiences that are not commonplace and taken for granted. You would expect strange things to happen there. You couldn't be certain whether these things would be good for you. You would surely be a bit apprehensive, perhaps a whole lot. You might wonder about your powers of endurance, your chances of survival. You might decide not to go there—if you had the choice. On the other hand, it might be just the place for you, right now.

The biblical writers take this image of the wilderness and develop it in three significant ways. First of all, it stands out from its surroundings as a special place, with sacred character. This is perhaps the chief reason why its physical appearance is so lightly touched upon—it is not what it looks like that really matters. This sacredness is ambiguous, for it can be the locus for God's providence or his wrath, either as a place from which to make a beginning, or as the place from which God will send the wind when he is going to destroy his people. Great signs and wonders occur there: the feeding with manna is one. It is a refuge for those who are rejected or unrecognized or persecuted—Moses hiding from Pharaoh,

David from Saul, Elijah from Jezebel, Jesus from the Pharisees. From the wilderness come the "words of life," the promise of the future. The end-time will begin there. And it is the wilderness that will eventually show forth God's glory, according to the prophet of the Exile and reaffirmed by all four evangelists.

Second, the wilderness is both the place and the occasion for a special relationship between people and God. With all the taken-for-granted comforts of the city and home life left behind, there is time and room for this relationship to emerge. The most striking thing about it is that it is holy: the people of the Exodus are referred to later as the holy desert assembly. There are other memorable aspects to this relationship: the idea of Israel as a wandering people seeking their land, and that of the wilderness as a testing place to try Israel's obedience to God. Israel is lost in the wilderness like sheep, and God the shepherd must guide them. Over all these tests or punishments, wanderings and individual retreats, there is the figure of God directly providing food and drink, direction, justice and vision; the opportunity to have direct communication with him is given to the few leaders he chooses.

Last, the wilderness becomes spiritualized by becoming metaphor— for the nation, the individual, and the city. The event that is chiefly associated with the wilderness, the Exodus, itself becomes metaphor for the supreme salvific act, the end of time, and the enduring reign of God.

There are three distinct strands to this metaphor. In the first, the wilderness lies somewhere between the promised land and Egypt, metaphorically as well as geographically. How the Hebrews view their situation, and how they choose to behave, determine whether they will go ahead towards the one or reverse their steps back to the other. For some— the ones who have faith—the wilderness is a proving ground and the occasion for the discovery of God's laws. For them it is the time of great miracles. Most people, however, see it as a death trap. They grumble, complain, rebel against God, worship idols, and despair of reaching the Promised Land. (They are the ones who don't make it.)

This behaviour—rebellion and apostasy—is used by the prophets to interpret subsequent misfortunes in the life of the Hebrews. On the opposite side, those writers who recall the sojourn as the time of "signs and wonders" remind a later people in captivity that God can and will deliver them mightily as he did before. So, by reflecting on the Exodus experience, they make of the sojourn in the wilderness a paradigm to which Israel can return.

In the second strand of the metaphor, the focus is on leadership, on the preparation of the individuals chosen by God, and on the new vision God presents to those who are called. The model hero is Moses, and in this strand those aspects of the wilderness life are emphasized that describe his call, his special relationship with God, and the vision that is given to him to present to Israel.

In the third strand of the metaphor a transvaluation of the wilderness takes place, and it takes on the traits of sinfulness. The image of the wilderness as infertile is used to refer to its geographical opposite, the city, and by extension to Israel, both land and people. Wilderness thus becomes a human condition, not a location in space. Because of the sins of the people, Judah and Israel are cast as moral wildernesses, and they will become worse—parched, devastated wastelands.

The grimness of the picture of the wilderness, however, is more than adequately overturned by the vision of its restoration to life and health. In this strand of the metaphor, not only is the wilderness itself changed, but in changing it God announces that he is doing something new, not simply returning Israel to the state of things in earlier exalted times. The new Exodus is a transcending of the old.

Through the wilderness will run a level way leading to Zion. On this road will walk the redeemed, those whom God is bringing back. On it God will walk in all his glory. The restored wilderness is also the metaphor for specific spiritual and material changes. It represents God's forgiveness of past sins and his promises of future justice, freedom, comfort. His spirit will be poured on his people and on their descendants. On the material side, Israel's enemies will be destroyed and her people will be brought back to their land.

The biblical wilderness and the stories told about it are all about remembering. Consider today in the light of the past. Are you miserable now? asks the prophet. Remember how God saved the people in the past. Think about your wicked ways today, and recall how God punished your ancestors. Have you turned away from God to follow other idols? Remember what happened in the wilderness of Sinai. Do you despair of being forgiven? Remember how many times God forgave the people who wandered away from him. Remember the signs and wonders of the past? Even more astonishing ones are promised. Do you see this wasted land, your ravaged cities? God has said they will be restored, made even more glorious.

People are constantly quoting the philosopher Santayana, who said that those who ignore history are bound to repeat it. It's not necessary to read philosophy to understand that. It's all here in the story of the ancient Hebrews, who made mistakes, misbehaved, promised to do better, were forgiven, and then repeated the cycle over and over. History is indeed important—when it suits us. At other times—well, there is God interrupting again to remind us.

Our memories are cunningly selective. We choose to remember what we need most. Usually it will be the good things: the champagne picnic recalled, the ants in the sandwiches forgotten. The best of times stay on, the worst of times too, but laundered, with much of the pain and anguish removed. I can remember, when I wish to, a particularly bad patch in my life, but I cannot revive the constant misery I felt, nor its acuteness. When we select, it is usually with the focus on "I." My children have told me about incidents in their youth that were horrid for them. I cannot remember them at all.

The Bible doesn't mince words or memories. Of course there's a good deal we don't know about the history of the Jews in their secular context. We don't know, for instance, what happened to the people in Palestine who had to give up their land for a promise made by YHWH— the Lord—a god they'd never heard of. How did God rationalize that one? Yes, it's true that every little tribe kept trying to run over the next one, but this little tribe—our religious ancestors—was supposed to be different, chosen for better things. The Bible, however, is not interested in all this. It tells the story of a struggle by an unruly, obtuse, obstinate bunch of ex-slaves to become the people of God. No wonder there were so many wildernesses to go through, both physically and spiritually, and that wilderness has remained such a powerful image throughout literature and history.

The rich complex that makes up the symbol of the wilderness in our culture appears in all its fullness in the biblical writings. Its prominent place in this literature allows us to see and unravel the strands that find their way into other early writings, whether they are inherited tales or sophisticated compositions, and into the literature of our own time. As

I will be examining some of these in the following chapters, I shall only say here that all the wildernesses encountered bear some resemblance to the archetypal wilderness I have been describing above, and that they are entered into by rare individuals such as those we have already met. In all these stories, the theme of the greatest importance is that of the deep and mysterious connection between the state of the wilderness and the condition of the human mind. This homology of land and person, as old as the Egyptian fertility myths, becomes the dominant relationship in many contemporary novels and plays.

In the well-known story from the Arthuriad of the Maimed King whose wound causes all the land to be made waste, it is the healing of the king that will restore the land. In today's less magical but just as mysterious view, the cure works in reverse: it is the wilderness that may cure the person's ills. On the other hand, just as Galahad by his purity calms the waters in the Forest Perilous, so heroes today, both live and literary, by their gracious vision and understanding may help to restore the land.

2

— WANDERING IN THE WILDERNESS —

Instead [the LORD*] led the people by the roundabout way of the wilderness to the Sea of Reeds.*

Exodus 13:18

Celia
But even if I find my way out of the forest
I shall be left with the inconsolable memory
Of the treasure I went into the forest to find
And never found, and which was not there
And perhaps is not anywhere? But if not anywhere,
Why do I feel guilty at not having found it?

T.S. Eliot, *The Cocktail Party*

"Wandering" is such a wonderfully open word. You cannot pin down one meaning for it, nor can you be sure when you see someone wandering that that is what is really going on. I watch my cat zigzaggedly beating the bounds of the garden, stopping to sniff, paw, scratch, or munch from time to time. Is he aimlessly cruising, or does he have a set purpose but a wiggly direction, or perhaps a well-considered path and no particular goal in mind? Other vignettes slide into my mind's eye: walking along a beach on the Dingle peninsula in Ireland with my cousin, collecting beautiful stones and shells. It wasn't our purpose in going there, but it became one. People wander around in shopping malls: looking for bargains, dates, or company, or just keeping out of the weather? People walking slowly and indecisively are often thought of as wandering—but they could be working out a complex menu for a party, or meditating on a sacred text.

Travel is our great excuse for wandering. Even if we have an itinerary planned in a general way, the best parts of the trip are those frequent times when we stray from the route, take the little lanes and follow a tiny local sign that says "To the lookout," or the monument, or the fountain. Some paths with no sign at all just have a certain intriguing feel to them, so we go to investigate and are usually not disappointed. (Ireland is perfect for this kind of wandering; so is France.)

It's more difficult to wander in daily life, because for most people, wandering has to be planned. (How's that for an oxymoron!) Just after I had my third child, a wise older friend told me to be sure and take off part of a day each week for myself, just to do nothing at all. I tried this: I went out to the woods for the afternoon, wandered along the trails and beyond, sat and read a book, drank some tea. It was bliss. The next week, and the next, it took me three hours each time to locate a babysitter who would come for the three-hour afternoon escape. I gave up. These days, while I do follow my cat around the garden every morning to see what is new, my physical wandering takes place mainly when I'm away from home. My mental wandering has no such holiday, but I won't go into that just yet.

While this sort of wandering in no-cellphone-land seems rather frivolous (although I don't really think that it is), it has none of the ultimate seriousness attached to the biblical idea of wandering in the wilderness. Picture the Hebrews' situation about 1300 BCE. When Joseph and his family had first gone to Egypt they were well-received, so others follow him to settle there. Now, under a new administration, the good times have turned to bad. The new pharaoh, Rameses II, has decided to re-build his capital city using the Hebrews as slave labourers. Perhaps others are pressed into service, too, but the Hebrews are in a truly rough spot because they have nowhere to go, even if they could escape their masters. Before they came to Egypt they had been a loose group of nomadic herdspeople, wandering for a living. But that was years ago. The later generations have become urbanized unskilled labour. That leaves them now homeless.

Their rescue begins when their God (not to be confused with the gods of the Egyptians) calls on one of them to be their leader, to take them out of Egypt. It takes Moses many visits to Pharaoh, and God many excruciating interventions—frogs and locusts and dead children and all—to convince Pharaoh of God's power and determination to free his people.

So Moses takes them into the wilderness, guided by God towards the land he has promised them, called Canaan. There is a direct way to Canaan along the coastal route, but it is busy and far too dangerous to take the Hebrews that way. Besides that, they need time learn what God wanted them to do. He intends to test and teach them, to find out who will be faithful to him, and to introduce the laws by which they are to govern their lives. He wants them to become an integrated community, his sacred people, not the ex-slaves and loosely connected nomads of the past. So he leads them by the longest possible way, to the south through the wilderness of Sin, where they stay for a long time, then up the east side through the wilderness of Paran to the north and to the wilderness of Zin. This journey lasts 40 years, so the story says; in other words, it takes a long time for this wayward people to learn, to ignore, to stumble, be reproved, be punished, repent, and start the process all over again until they are finally prepared for the new life of faith and true obedience to God in the Promised Land.

You could say that the Exodus experience is a period of trial and discovery, painful and frightening. There are very few places in the story where we hear of the Hebrews' joyful confidence or even timid optimism. Wilderness life cannot have been easy, even for the descendants of retired nomads. Despite that, Jeremiah's God calls it the honeymoon time:

> I remember the affection of your youth,
> the love of your bridal days:
> you followed me through the wilderness,
> through a land unsown. (Jeremiah 2:1-2)

The difference between a honeymoon and a trial of endurance depends on how well you are equipped to handle wilderness life, and more important, how you view the experience. Even though the Hebrews had no problems with survival—God looked after that—many distrusted the whole venture and wanted to turn back to Egypt. Hating every moment of the journey, they were anticipating trouble ahead. You could almost hear them saying, "The manna tasted all right, but who's to say we'll have enough tomorrow? We could starve right here in our tracks and no one would care." We don't read much about those who didn't complain, except that they were the ones God allowed to reach the goal. The others died along the way.

Although there are still a lot of wildernesses, near and remote, in which to wander today, what comes first to my Canadian mind when I think of wilderness is "up north," meaning somewhere around James Bay and beyond. (I used to think that "up north" meant any place two hours' drive north of Toronto, but I have learned better. It's pretty civilized there now.) Many Canadian novelists in the last century or so have written about "up north"; it seems to have been one of our consuming passions, for good or ill.

Rudy Wiebe's *A Discovery of Strangers* introduces us to two groups of wanderers with opposite views of the Canadian wilderness. Set in the Dene lands in what are now the Northwest Territories, the novel begins in 1820, at the time of John Franklin's overland trip from Hudson Bay to the mouth of the Coppermine River. Brought to the shore of Great Slave Lake by French-Canadian *voyageurs*, Franklin and his small British team meet a group of the Dene (called Tetsot'ine in the novel) and arrange with them to be escorted to the Arctic Ocean. Franklin intends to establish an overland route to the ocean, for the transport of furs to England.

The story, told from both sides, is of the coming together of these two groups of unlikely people, strangers to each other in every way. The narrative proceeds on the one side with the trials of Franklin's party, on the other with the sickness and death of Birdseye, the wise woman and seer of the Tetsot'ine. Woven between these tales is the viewpoint of the animals, as their own lives change both through natural causes and through the coming of "These English," as the Tetsot'ine call them. Central to the whole novel, and highlighting both the hopes and the impossibility of understanding between the English and the Tetsot'ine, is the gentle, pathetic love story of Robert Hood, the expedition's artist, and the beautiful Greenstockings, daughter of Birdseye and the shaman Keskarrah.

To be fair—and Wiebe is always that—the English are unprepared for the wilderness in winter. This is the coldest winter the Tetsot'ine can recall in a very long time. Greenstockings loves winter, because the snow smoothes out the land and she can run quickly on her snowshoes. The English do not have snowshoes; the Yellowknives, as the English call them, must eventually give them some. Even the *voyageurs*, who show Franklin's team how to build their log houses, do not grasp the arctic conditions. The clay with which they chink the logs cracks and falls off, letting the winds sweep through and keeping the English perpetually chilled. Hood is happily surprised at the comfort of the hide lodge where Keskarrah and his family live, sleeping naked under caribou skins.

The novel does not parade a simplistic confrontation of stereotypes. The five English explorers are as unalike as any group might be whose members' education levels, skills, and interests are so different. Seaman John Hepburn's pragmatic view of the events of the expedition is at odds with that of the lustful, ambitious, self-centred Midshipman George Back. Franklin's concern for order and Doctor Richardson's for accurate observation channel their judgments. Hood is the only one who sees the Tetsot'ine as people with needs like his own. His moral attitude annoys Back exceedingly.

Among the Tetsot'ine there is also a great diversity of characters. Bigfoot, who speaks for them to the English, is proud of the medal and the black hat that Franklin gives him. The English assume he is their leader, although the tribe does not have a leader, and gradually he begins to see himself that way. Broadface is as lusty in his way as is George Back, but he is an able hunter and good lover, not a promiscuous cheat like Back. Keskarrah, who has the "power to know something a little," is the one who dreams the caribou so that they will come to offer themselves as food for the tribe, who dreams the weather and the coming of snow and wind. His knowledge determines the movements of the Tetsot'ine, just as Franklin directs the English travels.

The Tetsot'ine give names to the English in much the same way as they have named each other: Franklin, short and stocky, is Thick English; Back, who is 24, is Boy English; Richardson becomes Richard Sun, and Hepburn is Hep Burn: because he roasts their meat to a blackened state, the Tetsot'ine, who boil theirs, think the name is amusingly suitable, as a name should be. Hood remains Hood, because he tries so hard to get Greenstockings to learn his name.

The novel is not about bad whites versus good Indians (or vice versa), although in the end my emotional divining rod leads me towards the latter. There is perhaps a slight underground polemical current, but not enough to dissuade one from taking the title seriously: the book is indeed about a discovery of what is strange. others, the characters themselves, the changing land. It is the land that is the most active participant, that drives the story, reveals the strangers, and offers the reader new thoughts to contemplate.

Although there are no stereotypes, there are sharp cultural differences between the two main groups. What one considers knowledge, the other believes is ignorance or misinformation.

The English look at the land as a vast, unknown, empty space that needs to be charted. It is cruel and mercurial. (How they can give it human characteristics when they are so busy otherwise deanimating it is an odd, contrary bit of characterization.) "God knows," says Back, "these natives live in a dreadful land with more than enough space quite empty around them." Placing his trust in numbers, Franklin, who has measured the temperatures during the previous October, cannot believe Keskarrah when he says that winter is here in August. Keskarrah, who goes by natural signs, doesn't understand why Franklin doesn't believe him:

> "The lake and river ice thundered cold at them the whole year they were carried to us." Keskarrah gestured to the passing wind. "Again and again. How much more did These English have to be told?"

It seemed they had heard only their own telling, as told to themselves.

To the Tetsot'ine the land is full—of places they know well, rocks, rivers, tall trees, small animals and, above all, of its own history:

> The stories the land told, Keskarrah said, and the sky over it in any place, were the stories of all People who had ever lived there, and therefore they were greater than any person, or two, could comprehend, even if one could have remained in one place motionless for an entire season, either of snow or mosquitoes.

The English, however, do not listen to the stories. They are mapping the territory, taking measurements and writing it all down. All this, says Keskarrah, is in vain:

> Nothing stays the way it is, everything changes when they come, and yet they mark it down as if it will always be the same and they can use it.... As if a lake or river is ever the same twice! When you

travel and live with a river or lake, or hill, it can remain mostly like it seems, but when you look at it with your dreaming eye, you know it is never what it seemed to be when you were first awake to it. Again and again Thick English talks about the Soul Everywhere, but he himself never looks for the sun. He and his men always stare at it through something else, and I think the sun uses their instruments to blind them. To make them think living things are always the same.

John Hepburn, while believing the land to be cruel, finds the people who live there quite the opposite. He says, "I think Mr. Hood understood better than anyone…how that beautiful land—so cruel no human being should ever live there, yet the Yellowknives do—could make a barbaric people so humane." Hepburn sees for himself how kind the Tetsot'ine are to the helpless explorers, who would have died without them, and how they care for the caribou. Keskarrah speaks his dismay to Broadface, who has been shooting the caribou to feed the English:

> ... endlessly pouring grey powder and poking a ball into an iron barrel, and flexing a finger on curled steel that can burn you raw, if you dare touch it, is not the way numberless beautiful caribou, who always will make it possible for human beings to live, should be forced to die. There is too much sacrifice being demanded. There is no consideration or tenderness left in so much long-distance killing; only noise and stink.

Underlying these differences is the contrast between the old wisdom and the new knowledge. Once again, the way in which the caribou are to be treated shows the contrast. The translator, Twospeaker, reports Keskarrah's words to Franklin:

> "He say, no deer now, by Copperwoman River. No deer now, by ocean. We dream here, quick, or everybody die, now. Women dry meat, scrape hides here."

> Lieutenant Franklin could not comprehend. "What does he mean, 'dream here'?"

> "The way they hunt."
> "Dreaming?"
> "Here, where deer maybe go."

"But they have guns now!"
"Guns…how to kill. Not hunt."
"What?"
"Dream, how you find 'em."

Franklin, who believes firmly in order, analysis, planning, thinks that there are ways and means to control the situation they are in, to arrange their travel even when Keskarrah says it is not good weather, and to force the Tetsot'ine, this disorganized group, to go with them. He is wrong on all counts. The Tetsot'ine, some of them, do go with the English, not because they are forced, but because they see it as a matter of hospitality: they have been asked to provide the English with food, so they will try to do so.

The Tetsot'ine way is one of acceptance of the land and the way of the caribou: all one can do is dream the things one wishes to happen, and hope that the land and animals consent. For the caribou are like themselves, though different in their ways. This is the song the hunters sing as they watch them arrive:

> How glorious to see,
> How unutterable, the great animals
> Who live by voices we may never hear.
> Another People like ourselves, splendid
> And complete, always travelling, always held
> Like we are in the magnificence and travail
> Of the long land.

Franklin observes unbelievingly that, despite their apparent lack of organization, the Tetsot'ine seem to outperform the *voyageurs*:

> Their ragged flotilla, where apparently every woman and child and man paddled or carried whatever as inclination moved them, had gradually, casually, outstripped his giant canoes and the voyageurs' contracted rhythm to vanish somewhere north over the rock shoulders of portages, across the endless hummocky, wet excretions of moss.

At the crux of all these differences of approach to the land, it would seem, are the two creation myths. Wiebe gives the telling of both of them to Keskarrah, with puzzled commentary by Greenstockings. With delightful irony, Judeo-Christian readers can see their story from the point of view of someone who, wise in his own ways, cannot fathom the peculiarity of such a tale. First the Tetsot'ine story: creation was born from the joyful union of Sky and Earth, who lay together and brought ground, trees, birds, caribou, and everything else out of their happiness. Man, who was cold and hungry in wintertime, was helped by a ptarmigan who lit his fire and made him snowshoes. When caught, she turned into a woman, and together they combined their skills to survive.

Then here is what Keskarrah discovers about the origins of the English: "Richard Sun said this to Bigfoot, I heard Twospeaker repeat it: 'You must know this, we men were made first from mud and the spit of the great Soul Everywhere.'" Because the English are using the white mud to chink their log house, Keskarrah suspects that this is some of the original mud, and that they should be called Whitemuds, even though they do not know that they came from here. One big problem for the English, as Keskarrah sees it, is the lack of cooperation between man and woman as reflected in their creation story:

> Richard Sun says woman Whitemud was supposed to be the companion and helper of the man. She happens out of his rib while he's sleeping, but when he wakes up and there she is, his rib a woman out of his sleep, she doesn't help him at all, she eats this one berry, which is so large it grows alone on one big tree, and then she gives it to him to eat and that makes everything in the world go completely crazy. Even the woman and the man.

Keskarrah interprets the Whitemuds' biggest problem: "For them the world is always wrong because they never want it to be...the way it is....Their first story tells them everything is always wrong. So wherever they go, they can see only how wrong the world is."

The novel does make me wonder what sort of a civilization we would have had if our creation story, like the Tetsot'ines', had been about cooperation, companionship, and joy, instead of about dominion, wrongdoing, and bleak survival. It is so hard to imagine whether people could be otherwise at the core of their being; we're so fixed in our belief that anger and fear breed violence, competition, separation, and woe. That is the way it has been and ever will be, world without end. It is human nature; as Samuel Beckett's Hamm says in *Endgame*, "You're on earth, there's no cure for that." Utopian writers have tried to persuade us otherwise, but we know that utopia means nowhere. The great Christian belief and hope is that people can be made new. Our original myth tells us why that is necessary. But still...can religion outdistance the culture that made it? I wonder.

Although I wouldn't make too much of it, there is a connection to be made in this novel between the wrongness of the world as the English see it, and their misfortunes, many of which are based on the inability to look and listen. The Tetsot'ine—those unstructured, casual people with supposedly no sense of time or direction—survive the heavy winter by sheltering and waiting. The English, with all their plans, become the wanderers, staggering overland when their canoes are smashed, after almost all the *voyageurs* die. During Hood's last days, when he and Richardson are reading the Bible together, they are deep in Leviticus, the book of laws that God gives to the Hebrews in the wilderness: ironically, the subject is wrongful sacrifice, a lesson that comes too late for Hood.

A third wanderer in the novel is Michel the lone Mohawk, who joins the *voyageurs* for unknown reasons, which eventually become clear. He is determined to kill the English, because whites, he claims, have brutally murdered and eaten his uncle and two brothers. He becomes more and more secretive and angry, almost insane; he attempts to rape Greenstockings and eventually kills Hood, who is almost dead already. Richardson kills him in turn. Michel is a Cain figure, an isolated wanderer distrusted by all the other groups; he certainly would have become a fugitive had he stayed alive.

Beneath all these contrasts, I think Wiebe is showing us a deeper, stronger bond that joins humans together. There is a delicacy of tone that he spreads over all his fictional beings, a light brushstroke of humankindness that includes even the stolid, unemotional Franklin and the roughcast *voyageurs*. You can even see into the wretched heart of Michel, victim turned attacker, and understand his torment a little. At times you can almost touch their fears—for example, those of Birdseye's family, as they watch the disintegration of her face, which they will never see whole again. They won't speak of it, though, just as Dr. Richardson and Hood will not let their dread of being left to freeze penetrate their decent English forbearance. The kindly love these two have for each other is there too, but unexpressed. Only Hood's sense of guilt and loss come tumbling through in his private dying thoughts. These are at the heart of the wilderness—fears of dislocation and of death, nostalgia for lost loves and dreams. Wiebe's world leaves me with a bittersweet feeling; I guess that is the kind of emotion you would expect to fill you in the wilderness.

The Tetsot'ine and the Hebrews of the Exodus period have this in common: they are both being led by supernatural means, whether it is the caribou seen in dreams, the land announcing the coming of winter, or a cloud by day and a pillar of fire by night. They are, in a sense, passive participants in the wilderness, wandering towards a goal, but never determining the way. The big difference between them is that, for the Hebrews, the wilderness is an undesirable means to an end, while for the nomadic Tetsot'ine it is home, one about to be dangerously disturbed by the newcomers. The Hebrews say, once we were slaves; now God is bringing us through the wilderness to our own fertile land. The Tetsot'ine could say, once we had a land we loved, but now we are being enslaved to others' ways, and our land is being destroyed. It must be remembered, however, that the Hebrews, in coming to Canaan, destroyed the peoples already living on the lands they passed through, so in this respect they have the same habits as "These English."

In fiction, as in some remarkable lives, people may be driven by altruism or love of God or some overwhelming insight or vision to follow their dreams in a truly dedicated fashion. Like the Arthurian knights, they are questers. A quest changes your life. It is utterly obsessive, compelling you to drop everything in your commonplace life and plunge ahead, knowing neither the time nor the place where you will arrive. Although I can't be sure of this, it seems that every quester goes warily or blindly through a wilderness of some sort. The route is never laid out, or direct. It may not even exist. In a recent issue of *Figaro Magazine*[3] I read about Philippe Valéry, a 33-year-old executive with Coca-Cola, who gave up his job to follow the silk and spice route from Marseille to China. He travelled 10,000 kilometres on foot, and took 784 days, following the route taken by Alexander the Great, Tamburlaine and Genghis Khan. He did it because he felt himself to be a "spectator of [his] own life." He wanted "to exist." I suppose you could say that Franklin, too, was a quester, though not on a sacred mission. The chief difference between him and Pierre, the next traveller we meet, is that the explorer thought he knew everything about his goal and the means to get there, whereas Pierre only gradually comes to understand what he is searching for.

The Canadian north is the primary setting in *La montagne secrète* (*The Hidden Mountain*), by Gabrielle Roy. You might say that in *A Discovery of Strangers*, as with the Exodus, the Tetsot'ine are being given a divine push from behind, while in Roy's novel the hero is being pulled forward. Not that I saw this sacred impulse at first: I thought this was going to be another story about self-discovery in the wilderness. Of course, I'm not alone; the hero thought so, too.

The physical journey begins in northern Saskatchewan, moves to Ungava, and ends in Paris. The hero's interior seeking began much earlier, before the present tense of the book, but is only resolved through the mediation of the wilderness. The traveller is Pierre, a man about whom we know practically nothing. We don't even learn his surname until five pages before the story ends. We don't know his background, except that he must have been raised in the north, because his father was a trader. We do not know why he has been travelling for ten years without discovering whatever it is that he yearns to know. He travels alone incessantly, by canoe and on foot. He sketches and paints as he goes, but we do not know whether he set out to learn to be a painter, or whether he just picked up the notion of painting and the skills for it along the way, as someone else might use a camera while travelling. Whatever his original reasons for painting, it takes on greater significance for him as he goes along, becoming finally his reason for living.

Because he is usually travelling alone, there is very little dialogue in the novel. This, coupled with the lack of particulars about Pierre's background and his usual life, makes him seem like a mythic hero. (He has no family, it seems, which for a man of his age is strange.) The narrative bears this out, because when you sum up his adventures at the end, they convey more to us than just the struggles of a young man to find himself in the north.

The physical appearance of the wilderness in *La montagne secrète* parallels the description of the biblical one. It is unsown land, both flat and mountainous, bearing grass and vegetation in some places, barren and rocky in others. It varies as Pierre travels from forest to the tree line, to the hills and valleys of southern France. The Ungava landscape is described as "an expanse of sterile steppes, punctuated by countless shallow lakes, where one can journey for days on end without seeing anything except the eternal moss underfoot and, far away, the flat and baffling horizon."

Vast and empty, too, is the plain near Marseille: "He saw the long plain of Crau, flat as the sea; a motionless plain extending to infinity and covered with so many pebbles that one's mind was lost in wonder: whence can have come so odd a deluge?"

Because Pierre is visually drawn to the landscape, his wilderness is much more nuanced and colourful than is the biblical one, which exists perhaps more for its meaning than its being. Pierre the artist is absorbed by the changing seasons, the diminishing of vegetation as he goes north. He differs from the biblical writers in that he finds beauty in the wilderness; even in the midst of bare, stony ground he is overwhelmed by the carpeting of red flowers. "But would he ever forget," he thinks, "the astounding color of these flowers, and would he ever lose his longing to see them once again?" Biblical writers, when they notice their surroundings, point only to the waste and carnage.

The people who live in Roy's wilderness are nomads, hunters, and trappers who follow the herds. They shelter, as did the children of Israel, in tents. They shelter Pierre. One winter he spends with Steve Sigurdson, helping him with his traps and painting when going outside is impossible. Another winter is spent in the village of the Eskimo Orok, where Pierre recovers from fatigue and overexposure in Ungava. Although there are dangerous animals in the wilds, the emphasis here is not upon their ferocity but upon their suffering. Pierre and Steve discover a trapped mink that has chewed its own leg in an attempt to escape. Pierre draws the exhausted sled dogs lying in a heap. The other hazards one may encounter are worse than the threat of fierce animals: there is the chance of sudden storms, starvation, unmanageable rapids, sickness, exposure.

Pierre is seeking something important, but we—and he—don't know what it is. All we know is that he has some inner compulsion to find out "what the world would have of him—or he of the world." Sometimes he thinks that his vocation is humble, as when he tries to draw the frail poplar that he believes to be the furthest north of its kind. "Perhaps," he muses, "there was nothing more involved than the job of making this individual tree distinct from all other trees, to be the author of its revelation." At other times he senses a grander revelation to come, hearing "the summons of a beauty that did not yet exist, but which, were he ever to reach its realization, would engulf him in an incomparable happiness." He is not wrong; the summons he imagines will come, and it will change his life.

As Pierre travels, his attachment to nature becomes more and more intense. He associates people and trees—sometimes only in a visual way, but more often as kinfolk. He changes an "as if" similarity into a "we together" one. Here are the trees in transformation. First they appear "only in tiny, isolated groves, almost black against the rocky soil, and [take] their stands like knots of people gathered here and there by chance in the wilderness." Then there is the beginning of an association: "Around them nothing took on any clarity of outline in the dreamlike half light; men and trees seemed almost indistinguishable from each other; there were times when you might have thought the men were standing still while the trees moved cautiously onward." In the beginning of this journey, Pierre has ascribed human thought to a solitary aspen—"the little tree gave you the impression of deeply pondering its own forthcoming demise." Yet at the close of his life, Pierre himself, who is tall and bent like a spruce, has become treelike. "As he listened to these words, Pierre visibly brightened. First a roaring had begun in his ears. Then to the face so long closed and constrained there mounted something like the sap of spring; the tree, from its distant roots, at last drawing life."

These thoughts may be seen simply as those of a lonely artist trying to put a human face on a strange and disturbing landscape. But Roy takes her hero even further in this fierce and startling relationship with the wilderness. The momentum has been building, from Pierre's first ruminations about the suffering of nature—the mink, the poplar—to his sense that something "strange and cold in all its splendor" will be revealed to him. The two most overpowering experiences of his life take place in quick succession in Ungava.

One evening as Pierre prepares to make camp after an exhausting day, he is disturbed by unhappy memories; and by the sadness of not having accomplished anything worth doing. At the same time he is invested with the belief that something marvellous is going to occur. He picks up his canoe, climbs around a rock wall and discovers his mountain.

Before him towered a high and solitary mountain that glowed in the red sunlight and burned brilliantly like a great pillar of fire.... It was proud—incomparably proud—and incomparably alone. Fashioned to please the eye of an artist in its planes, its dimensions, its colors; and it had chosen, moreover, to reveal itself in its most glorious hour.

Pierre stands in awe and wonder:

...thus from the beginning of time had his mountain existed; not in vain had he sought it; it truly was, really existed, and he at last had found it. There he stood now, scarcely larger than a speck of dust as compared to that mighty mass; nonetheless it seemed to him that the mountain was pleased he should be looking at it, and that it spoke to him.

He begins to sketch the mountain, a portion of it at a time. His efforts give him great delight, but he comes to realize that he would be even happier if someone could see them. He sees that he has done his work for others, not just for himself. He imagines himself holding a captive bird inside him that needs to be freed. "'But,' thought Pierre, 'whenever he himself set himself free, did he not, by that very fact, also set other men free, set free their imprisoned thought, their suffering spirit?'" This is his first step in turning towards others with something to offer them.

Pierre becomes so engrossed in his work that he does not notice that the weather is closing in, and he is running out of food. At this moment he sees an old caribou standing alone, probably, he thinks, left behind by the herd, and certain to die. He gives chase, and in the lengthy tracking that follows, Pierre wounds the animal several times. As they both become exhausted, he travels along with it, resting when it rests. The caribou makes him angry because it will neither die nor allow him to kill it. As the chase drags on, the two share the same suffering, fatigue, and, finally, thirst. Pierre mercifully allows the caribou to drink before he kills it. He sinks down to sleep beside the dead animal, allowing its warmth to sustain him: "In the endless stretches of the tundra they formed a tiny, motionless, almost fraternal patch of shadow."

In the pursuit and killing of the caribou, Pierre has experienced the suffering of all creatures, and the interrelatedness of the hunter and the hunted. "Now, having warmed him, the caribou was to become for him flesh, blood, and his very thought." As he eats some of the flesh of the caribou, he cries over "this dreadful part of creation, its cold, its unbearable harshness."

This intermingling of the two visions, of the beauty and majesty of the world and of the suffering that comes with living in it, sustains Pierre, and leaves him haunted by the desire to express them. During his recuperative stay with Orok's tribe, Pierre meets the missionary Father Le Bonniec, who encourages him to exhibit his paintings and persuades him to go to Paris to study. Pierre takes his wilderness with him: his studio in Paris becomes a replica of his shelter in Ungava, his memories of Ungava come to inform his life, and even his paintings of Paris have an arctic tone. As he paints he feels as if he were lifting a canoe for a portage. Eventually he decides to paint a self-portrait. He gives it antler-like forms on its head, and an expression of "unbearable lucidity and sadness." In viewing it his friend Stanislaus asks, "Was this not that high-pitched lament in which are commingled the anguish of killing and of being killed?"

Perhaps it is this self-recognition that permits Pierre at the end to have a vision of his mountain again, and to begin to paint it.

> Suddenly there passed over him so blissful a tremor of delight that he stood stock-still, awaiting the image that was breaking through the fog, gliding toward him like a loved one.

> The resplendent mountain was once more before him.

As he is putting the perfect colour on his painting, Pierre has a heart attack and dies. His last thought is the fading vision of his mountain. "Who, in the mists would ever find it again?"

Roy's novel is a fine description of how the wilderness may bring new understanding and hence new life to those who search for it. The wilderness teaches Pierre that beauty alone is not enough. It is accompanied by suffering, the agony and the ecstasy together. Beauty without meaning is of no use to anyone except the experiencer, and even there it is diminished where understanding is missing. Pierre's art teacher in Paris corrects his view of art, which is at the same time his view of life. "It is not because the mountain is beautiful that you should make a painting of it. What has a lovely mountain got to do with painting?" Stanislaus amplifies this remark with his idea that a painter defines the inner resonance of the universe. Pierre begins to see that one's job is not to record the naturally beautiful—to replicate experience—but to give it meaning, for then the subject of art can be anything; all of life resonates once the painter shows it. From his beginning as a solitary person with a vision he cannot and does not wish to share, he becomes a painter for others, leaving a legacy of his paintings to those who have shown him kindness. The solitary visionary has the makings of the prophet.

How do you know a wilderness? The preservation or reclamation of the earth's wild spaces has become a frontline political issue rather than the bizarre lament of a bunch of goofy tree-huggers. What happens next—how the wilderness is treated—depends on how it is seen, felt, and understood. Looking at the literature I have discussed so far, you see how varied these approaches can be. In the West the biblical tradition has had the greatest influence. The wilderness and its inhabitants are seen as distinctly different from us; in fact, one wouldn't even try to make a comparison, for there is little basis for it. As in the Bible, we see it as a place to go for specific reasons: to escape, to hide, to slog through en route to a distant goal. Either it's a necessary evil, or it's in the way.

For some, though—those early explorers, contemporary trippers—it has been an overwhelming experience of discovery, just as it was for some who lived through the 40 years on the way to Canaan. For these, the wilderness has the power to change lives. So it is for Pierre, the solitary artist, but his (or Roy's) view of the wilderness is very different from the biblical one, almost animistic. Pierre knows the wilderness in full romantic dress, as affecting his emotions and guiding him, as almost like himself in its struggles and feelings. Here, for instance, is the first shaft of sunlight after a dark winter in northern Saskatchewan:

> It reached his cheek and lingered there like a child's caressing hand. At the contact of this living warmth, without reflecting yet as to its cause, he felt his wretchedness melting within him, felt his blood move again in his veins, felt his flesh come back to life. It was as though he were healed by a touch of tenderness, of something at last that knew pity.

As he follows the wounded caribou, the land itself seems to suffer as he and the animal do. "He...found himself in an intricate network of grotesque rock masses, though they were of no great height. In what strange corner of creation was he? What could be the meaning of such a monstrous tangle of tormented, almost suffering stone?" Roy is pushing the Wordsworthian envelope a bit too far for this Westerner (I do not know whether even a Buddhist would agree that stones are tormented), but it is certainly a common experience to associate our moods with the weather, the landscape, the time of day.

The English explorers in *A Discovery of Strangers*, not surprisingly, know the wilderness, as did their biblical forebears. It is a cruel place where hardship occurs. They see it as distinctly "other," to be conquered, used, and perhaps destroyed, a future envisaged by the Tetsot'ine seers. This is of course the strain of understanding that we have been accustomed to over the centuries, although we modify it by our fondness for the cute little otters and the graceful deer. In Wiebe's novel, however, we are offered another vision of the wilderness, one of kinship with difference. Unlike Pierre's response, which is to give everything he sees the emotions he is feeling, the Tetsot'ine recognize that each part of nature has its own inner life, that all, though different in kind, are held together in this green and living world. As Pierre receives help from the sun, so the caribou will help people to survive, but in their own time and way. The idea of "dreaming" the caribou is totally foreign to white Westerners: to allow nature its own place in the world and to meet its needs, not ours.

It looks as though there are as many ways of wandering in the wilderness as there are ways of moving your body. If, for instance, you are a true quester, you will know what your goal is—to find the Golden Fleece, the Holy Grail, the lost sheep, even—and you will wander purposively until you reach it. If you are among the children of Israel, you may continue faithfully on your quest to reach the Promised Land, or you may give up part way along, finding this wandering life too hard, and longing for the fresh fish and melons of Egypt. If you are John Franklin, you will never give up, counting it a matter of duty and honour, and believing that your rational approach to the wilderness will succeed.

All these questers are clear about their goals, even those who refuse to persevere. Then there is Pierre, a dedicated traveller, who has a great desire to achieve his goal but doesn't know exactly what it is. His wandering is self-discovery in motion, and his undirected travelling parallels his slow and gradual recognition of who he is and what is his vocation. The questions "Who am I?" and "Who are you?" (directed at the animals, suffering beings like himself) and "Where is here?" are brought together, as the wilderness teaches him the answers. The connection between the wilderness and one's inner condition is not a new one: Terry L. Burden, referring to Psalm 119:176, says that in it "the period of the forty years of wandering in the wilderness is restated as a wandering of the heart...."[4] In such solitary places, self-doubt and new insights are possible and probable.

Wandering with a goal is one thing; aimless wandering is quite another, and it is that which seems to me to characterize much of Western society. Now that both religion and its chief ideological alternative, Marxism, are at a low point in the West, there is a hollowness, a kind of wilderness, where all familiar landmarks have been ignored or obliterated. There are some sectarian attempts to put a fence around this unruly space and to set up barriers, simplistic signposts, even altars to ancient gods. These are fraudulent ways of disguising the untidiness of the real world, which is for the most part uncharted ground, bleak, but also sometimes beautiful.

Another kind of wandering has no goal and no direction, and is often as much physical as psychological or spiritual. This is the sorry life of anomic people, or people whose minds are ill at ease, or people who have no home and no function in society. We will meet a fictional group of wanderers like this in the next chapter.

Pierre, who sets out as a mystified wanderer with an uncertain goal, becomes a kind of Moses figure. Like Moses, he spends years in the wilderness seeking his goal but is unable to take a direct path towards it. Like Moses, Pierre is nourished and sheltered by an external source. At times he has the sense of being led, a sense that occasionally becomes suspect to him. He has his mountain, his Sinai experience. In Paris he sees it again, transformed, made his own. In a sense he has a glimpse of the Promised Land, but like Moses, he remains behind in the wilderness. He is not the one to enter in and enjoy it, although he has played his part in leading others towards it.

Wandering can have its dark and its light sides. To be lost—that is, unable to find a path you need—can be truly frightening. Once I was in northern Algonquin Park as part of a group of canoe trippers who came into a very large lake, deeply scalloped with bays and inlets. In late afternoon we tried to find a suitable campsite, but all the shores we passed were steep rock cliffs. Landing was impossible. As it grew dark, I began to panic, but our leader seemed calm. Eventually, in the pitch-black darkness of a 30-metre-deep lake, we bumped up against a shore line that seemed like a rough climb, but accessible. We hauled our sleeping bags up to the top, found a flattish place, and went to sleep. In the morning we discovered it was a beautifully laid-out campsite, and as we saw later, the only one at that end of the lake. The thought of that night still makes me shiver. It was the first time that the idea of dying ever entered my head, of falling asleep in that unresisting blackness and tumbling into the water. If this seems like overreacting, try to remember how it was to be sixteen and terrified. In the daylight, looking at that impregnable shore and the danger we were in, I knew my fear was justified.

In everyday life we'd rather not wander. We want to put down straight lines, because it's safe, and it saves time. I'd much rather be able to go directly to my friend's house, rather than wander around the neighbourhood guessing which is the right turn for her street. Straight lines mean that you know your way; you remember. Wandering means that you are continually asking questions. But if you put down a straight path in the forest so you can go through it the easiest way, how many trees do you have to cut down to make the path? How much of life's greenery do we step on or ignore while beelining it to the next goal? I do it all the time. I do it all the time, along with Franklin and all our kind.

The light side of wandering is what I have loved in these books: discovery, revelation, even nurturing. One mustn't forget the manna, the meeting of strangers in kindness, the caribou as food, even the discovery of the perfect campsite. The unexpected gifts of the wilderness.

My serious adult wanderings are mental ones. They take place in a theological forest, always musing but never settling anything—or so it seems to me. The wilderness of Anne has no trail pointing the best way, and not many fresh signs to hint at what it might be. There are lots of worn, overgrown trails, even some well-kept, solid-looking ones, but they are not for me. There are signs pointing to places I would not go. There are some way-stations, but the water there is rather tasteless, the bread dry. I wander, not in a "haze of faith," as A.L. Kennedy puts it, but only in a fog of uncertainty. Sometimes, like Pierre, that passion for the overwhelming is aroused—desired, but not realized.

Sometimes I can form the right questions that could lead me out of the wilderness. Then I wonder if they are the real questions after all. I ask how a woman who believes in and expects equality and collegiality among people can stay within a hierarchical structure that still proclaims, here or in the ether, that father knows best. How can I repeat words that confirm the patriarchal construction of the universe, of society, of my little worshipping group? Why say what I don't mean? Then, glancing down another little trail, I think, don't be a Franklin, drawing up firm lines of truth and falseness, actual and make-believe. Somewhere, somehow, out of the old truth, the new will emerge. Wait and wander.

Wandering, seeking, plodding, getting lost, finding, slowing down, bitching, foot-dragging, mind-bruising, resting, reviving, trudging, musing, dead-ending, giving up, not giving up, resuming wandering…such is the manner of going through the wilderness. It seems that the material scene propels the inward one—or perhaps it is vice versa. One doesn't go into the wilderness as a *tabula rasa*; we bring our solitariness, our deepest questions, our howling agony with us into whatever bare plain, rugged mountain, or dark woodlands we enter, either in fact or in imagination. The wilderness is in us and all about us.

3

— A PLACE FOR THE PARIAH —

I am like an uprooted tree, dying at the core....

Anna Brownell Jameson, *Winter Studies and Summer Rambles in Canada*

The invisible world, he declared to himself, had abandoned him as a gypsy soul to wander singular, without guide or chart, through a broken world composed of little but impediment.

Charles Frazier, *Cold Mountain*

I n 1948 I saw a film that chilled me from head to toe. It was *The Snake Pit*, starring Olivia de Havilland in a difficult and heart-wrenching role that should have won her the Academy Award. (Apparently Jane Wyman's role in *Johnny Belinda* as a deaf-mute who murders the man who raped her affected the jurors even more. This must have been the year of the abused woman.) The story tells of a woman who has gradually been overtaken by delusions and paranoia, and is thrown into a mental hospital for good or ill. The effect of the film wasn't felt just by someone of an "impressionable age"; older and more experienced moviegoers were shocked at this realistic, sometimes ferocious look at mental illness. In one scene, from which the film probably gets its name, the heroine is standing in a room where the inmates are wandering about, circling, muttering and moaning, each one isolated from the other in her particular hell or vacant tomb. The room resembles a pit full of snakes coiling and uncoiling themselves.

That is one scene that is printed on my memory with indelible ink. The other, which still brings tears, is of a concert in the hospital, at which one of the patients, out of the deep enclosure of her lost self, sings a solo, which is reprised, in the sentimental film fashion of the time, by the whole group of patients. The melody is the Largo from Dvořák's *New World* symphony; the song is called "Going Home." I believe that the melody was inspired by a Negro spiritual. The poignancy of this scene, with its terrible irony, its tremulous hopefulness sliced through by bitter reality, haunts me whenever I hear the *New World.*

In the context of this film, this song, it is even difficult right now to think about what "home" means. For me it has always meant safety, stability, a place to pull back into when the going is tough. It is also a place of love and beauty, but the sheltering part comes first. I suppose that is because we moved so often when I was a child. By the time I was 13, I had gone to seven schools and lived in as many dwellings in four cities. I don't remember the shifts in town and house and school as particularly traumatic—except for one horrid experience in Toronto in Grade 3 where I was made to feel that I was the dunce of the class —but I do remember the great excitement when I was 15 and we moved into a house of our very own, out of the rented apartments we had been in up till then. Since that time, I have been fortunate enough to have had a "real" home, and I have worked hard to make it as welcoming for body and soul as possible.

The search for home is one of the deepest quests of all, the expulsion from home the gravest loss. In one way or another many of us are on a perpetual quest to find home, some to return to a home from which they have been thrown out and to start again, some to find a better place than the one they have left. The ancient Hebrews were in both camps. Some wanted to go back to Egypt, a place where they had been enslaved but still felt safer than on this shapeless journey with who knew what outcome. Others wanted dearly to reach the Promised Land, their new, true home. All of them had been led into the wilderness by one they should have trusted utterly with their lives—their God.

Some biblical figures were not led into the wilderness but were driven there by force or circumstance. Most notable of these refugees is the prophet Elijah. Right from the start Elijah seems to have been uprooted. The most famous stories about him tell of his altercations with King Ahab, who lived in Samaria, on the west side of the Jordan. To reach him, Elijah would have had to leave his old home in Gilead, east of the river. He seems never to have had a permanent home throughout his prophetic career. On the most threatening occasion, when he confronts Ahab, he has to escape his pursuers by going deep into the wilderness. The story is one of the great dramatic events in the Bible. It makes one realize why Elijah would have been a most disturbing neighbour, even at some distance.

Ahab is married to the infamous Jezebel, daughter of the king of Sidon, who is a Baal worshipper. Consequently she murders (personally? the story doesn't say) all the prophets of God she can get her hands on. She doesn't catch Elijah. After warning Ahab that God is furious at him for this show of apostasy, Elijah proposes a test. Bring out all your 400 prophets of Baal to Mount Carmel, he says. We shall have two altars, one for them and one for me. Place your sacrifice—a bull—on the altar, build up the fire, but don't light it. Then call on Baal to set it on fire. You go first.

All day the prophets dance around the altar, calling out for Baal, shouting and gashing themselves with their swords and spears—reminds me of *The Snake Pit*—egged on by Elijah, who says, "Call louder, for he is a god: he is preoccupied or he is busy, or he has gone on a journey; perhaps he is asleep and will wake up." Nothing happens. Then Elijah takes his turn—and you know what comes next. God lights the fire immediately, and all the people fall down and praise him. Elijah takes the 400 prophets away and slaughters them. (No assistants are mentioned.) It is no wonder that Jezebel is enraged and threatens to kill him; Elijah escapes into the wilderness, where he spends 40 days and nights walking to Horeb, the holy mountain. What happens there is another story.

While Elijah is a mighty prophet to whom God speaks directly, in the pursuit of his vocation he is a religious and political outsider, going against the ruling house of Israel. He must hide for fear of reprisals, and the biblical hiding place is almost always the wilderness. So, in the first instance, the wilderness is a protective shelter; in the second, it is a place in which to make overwhelming new discoveries. One may not always feel safe in this dangerous place, but it is safer than in the city.

Charles Frazier's *Cold Mountain* introduces a hero who is also an outcast, hiding for his life, although he is no Elijah. A young man from Cold Mountain in North Carolina, Inman has fought in the Civil War and was wounded in a battle outside Petersburg, Virginia. Against all odds, he has recovered in hospital sufficiently to know he will be sent back into the fray. One night he walks out of the hospital and into the woods to begin his long trek home. After plodding through many sorts of rough terrain, encountering hardened villains and kindly outsiders, he reaches his goal, only to have it snatched away from him.

Inman's story is only one thread of this intricately woven novel. The second story is about Ada Monroe, daughter of a minister who has recently died, leaving her in possession of a derelict farm and a large parcel of land, which she is completely unskilled to handle. She is rescued by Ruby, whose ne'er-do-well father has gone off to the war. Ruby, wise in the ways of farming and of nature lore, trains Ada to take responsibility for her land and farm, and together they gradually turn it into a flourishing homestead.

Weaving these two stories together is the love between Inman and Ada. Inman can hardly think of anything else but the hope that, when he sees Ada again, she will agree to marry him. Ada is not so obsessed— she is too much taken up with her new occupations—but she cherishes every letter from him and the few memories of their loving moments together. When they do finally meet, the love and tenderness they have for each other is equally given.

More narrative threads fill out the pattern. There is Ruby's reconciliation with her father, Stobrod, wonderfully reformed. Told as memory is Ada's story of her life with her father, from their arrival at Cold Mountain. Stitched between these longer narratives are the episodic adventures Inman has along the way, among the most significant of which are the meeting with the young widow Sara; another with the goat woman, maker of simples; and the encounter with the bear and her cub.

This is a war story split in two. On one side are the deserters hiding from both the Federal soldiers who want to kill them and the vicious Home Guard bent on bringing them back either to prison or to fight again. There's a cameo about one of the nastiest characters—a farmer who turns people in for the bounty. On the other side are the women, alone and abandoned as a result of war or death. The novel doesn't play on this theme with a feminist drumbeat, though. Such situations must divide the sexes here, since women in the 1860s do not fight battles. Women in the country often perform the same tasks as men, war or no war. For Ada and Ruby it is push the plow, build the fence, or quit.

Above all, it is the wilderness that looms fair or foul throughout the novel. It is not a single image: there are as many wildernesses in the book as there are stories, bearing all shades and sentiments. The images are weighted heavily on the dismal and horrific side, from the dark and fearsome forest to the wasted lands after battle. They appear, sometimes pathetically, sometimes with hope, as the locus for Inman's survival. And they point timidly to the possibility of a restored postwar world where life can again be lived in harmony with nature.

Ada's first trip from Charleston to Cold Mountain with her father makes her uneasy, as she fears the road will peter out, "leaving them adrift in a wilderness as trackless and profound as that which leapt up when God first spoke the word *greenwood*." Her Charleston friends think the mountain region is "a heathenish part of creation, outlandish in its many affronts to sensibility, a place of wilderness and gloom and rain where man, woman, and child grew gaunt and brutal, addicted to acts of raw violence with not even a nod in the direction of self-restraint." However, their opinion is proven wrong: Ada grows to love her little farm in the wilderness so much that when her father dies she decides to stay, even though she has no idea how she will survive.

Ruby's first powerful experience of the wilderness takes place when she is four years old, and she is forced to spend the night alone in the woods beside the river, her nightgown caught on a blackthorn, because there was no one at home to come to her rescue. Terrified that animals will come and eat her, she is soothed by a voice, "some tender force of landscape or sky, an animal sprite, a guardian that took her under its wing and concerned itself with her well-being from that moment on." Left on her own most of the time as a child (she doesn't even know her mother), Ruby comes to know the mountains "as intimately as a gardener would his bean rows," and knows how to make her life among them, confident that she is protected.

A lonely, remote wilderness is inhabited by the goat woman, who shelters and feeds Inman on his journey home. It is an ugly place with misbegotten trees: "Inman could imagine the place in February with a howling downhill wind driving snow sideways among the bare trees." The kindly old woman prefers this isolation to her previous life. Sold by her family to a mean and demanding husband who has killed off three wives with overwork, she escapes here to live in a caravan and breed her goats.

There is the desolate wilderness of the abandoned Cherokee village, where Ada and Ruby stay to nurse Ruby's wounded father, and where Inman finds Ada. Like the lives of its former inhabitants, the village is wasted and empty, "a ghost town, its people long since driven out onto the Trail of Tears and banished to a barren land." Inman and Ada remember these outcasts: "Those people's fears had been fully realized. The wider world had found them, even hidden here, and had fallen on them with all its weight."

Mainly it is Inman's wildernesses that permeate the novel. More than landscape setting or cause of action, they intrude on and stir his thoughts, colour his moods, inspire his hopes, and dampen his soul. As he makes his long, slow way through rough terrain back to Cold Mountain, he considers the depressing state of the world, makes difficult ethical choices, and sways between cynical despair and faint hope.

War is what has driven him to view the world so bleakly. As he is walking through foul country, filled with the black stumps of burned trees, he recalls the battlefield the day after the fighting. "The land lay bleak as a nightmare and seemed to have been recast to fit a new and horrible model, all littered with bodies and churned up by artillery." The two views, of burnt trees and mutilated bodies, are similar. Even though there are lovely aspects of nature that he still recognizes, war has made him an outsider, unable to unite himself with them.

> But sooner or later you get awful tired and just plain sick of watching people killing one another for every kind of reason at all…. So that morning he had looked at the berries and the birds and had felt cheered by them, happy they had waited for him to come to his senses, even though he feared himself deeply at variance with such elements of the harmonious.

For the most part Inman does not see the beauty, if beauty there is. He travels through flatwoods of "trash trees," then through a forest of scrub pines, "a sick and dangerous place." The river is "foul as the contents of an outhouse pit," a "smear on the landscape." As he walks at night, his fear makes him think every tree is a threatening person, and the forest's noises seem to be coming "from the jangle of his own troubled mind." Trying to escape from gunshots by floating down the malodorous river, he imagines a gigantic catfish swallowing him, "his life adding up to no more than catfish droppings on the bottom of this swill trough of a river."

Inman's path through the wildernesses is never clear nor straight, although he knows he must head generally west. He takes the round-about hidden ways, travels at night, climbs in fog, and once, when he is captured, is led back in the opposite direction to his home. Later on, he finds himself "fuddled and wayless." At another time he thinks he is probably travelling in circles, "So he went blindly through the fog, taking whatever tack he felt at that moment to be west, and tried to make himself content with just motion."

Although the story takes place in autumn, the prevailing colour is black, the temperature chill. Right from the start of the book, the miserable hospital is decorated with black detailing: the flies on the ceiling, the black mushrooms that grow daily on Inman's book in the air so damp it felt "like breathing through a dishrag," the lank black hair of his dying neighbour. Worst is his recurring dream following the battle of Fredericksburg, a dream so hideous that Inman awakes "in a mood as dark as the blackest crow that ever flew." His black mood carries on, through the landscape covered with blackened stumps of burnt trees, through the fog in which only the black trunks of trees can be seen. In his lowest state, starved and crawling on his hands and knees towards a creek, Inman sees a wet crow that sits "hunched and ill looking." The sight brings him to his feet. Black birds appear everywhere in the story—ravens, crows, vultures.

Black dominates in two of the most painful episodes. As Inman and the other captured men are being led along roped together, one of the Guards knocks off their hats; "any man who bent to pick up his hat was beat with the stock end of the gun. They walked on leaving fifteen black hats lying in the road as spoor of their passage." On another day Inman is faced with a black bear and her cub. Believing that he must never kill another bear, from whom he might learn how to live peaceably, he is the unavoidable cause of her death. Then, rather than leave the cub to starve, he shoots it. "Even my best intentions come to naught," he thinks, "and hope itself is but an obstacle."

At every step of the way through this dreary and frightening landscape, Inman's thoughts are of Cold Mountain. He compares wherever he is with his home, and only the possibility of settling there makes him think he can be restored. "Cold Mountain nevertheless soared in his mind as a place where all his scattered forces might gather." (One can imagine Elijah clutching a similar thought as he tramps to Mount Horeb.) Inman's fondest imaginings include Ada.

> He thought of getting home and building him a cabin on Cold Mountain so high that not a soul but the nighthawks passing across the clouds in autumn could hear his sad cry. Of living a life so quiet he would not need ears. And if Ada would go with him, there might be the hope, so far off in the distance he did not even really see it, that in time his despair might be honed off to a point so fine and thin that it would be nearly the same as vanishing.

When he finally sees Cold Mountain, he is in a more downcast mood, yet it still is a refuge for him. "Surely off in that knotty country there was room for a man to vanish. He could walk and the wind would blow the yellow leaves across his footsteps, and he would be hid and safe from the wolfish gaze of the world at large." Finally, in their last times together, he and Ada plan a life beside Cold Mountain, their version of a land of promise. Soon after, however, Inman is shot and dies near a black creek.

It shouldn't surprise anyone that Inman is killed just as he seems to be nearing the end of his solitary journeying. From the moment he walks out of the hospital he has been given a different identity—a deserter, no longer a human with rights, thoughts, and feelings, but a prey to be trapped. His view of the world since he has been in battle goes from cynicism to despair, sometimes mitigated by faint hope that things will change. He has seen "the metal face of the age, and had been so stunned by it that when he thought into the future, all he could vision was a world from which everything he counted important had been banished or had willingly fled." Not only does he hold little hope for the world, he sees how he has become diminished:

> His spirit, he feared, had been blasted away so that he had become lonesome and estranged from all around him as a sad old heron standing pointless watch in the mudflats of a pond lacking frogs. It seemed a poor swap to find that the only way one might keep from fearing death was to act numb and set apart as if dead already, with nothing much left of yourself but a hut of bones.

He compares his lot with that of the wandering show folk, gypsies and outliers—all nomads like himself. Since he has been fighting, his view of the war has changed: "All I know is anyone thinking the Federals are willing to die to set loose slaves has got an overly merciful view of mankind." And he disagrees with General Lee's view, which sees war "as an instrument for clarifying God's obscure will.... Inman worried that following such logic would soon lead one to declare the victor of every brawl and dogfight as God's certified champion." If you win, you are right—an argument that even today drives hard-line theists to war to prove this belief over and over again.

Even while lying beside Sara, a widow with a frail baby, Inman still despairs of his own recuperation. He cannot put out a hand to comfort her: "It was his lot to bear the penalty of the unredeemed, that tenderness be forevermore denied him and that his life be marked down a dark mistake." He imagines life with Ada and their grandchildren, but thinks it an unlikely prospect. Both the universe and his spirit have been distorted.

> But to believe such an event might actually happen required deep faith in right order. How would you go about getting it when it was in such short supply? ... You could be too far ruined. Fear and hate riddling out your core like heartworms. At such time, faith and hope were not to the point. You were ready for your hole in the ground.

On Inman's side of the story, the mood is dark, like the war, like the wilderness. It is lightened only by his innate kindness and clear, ruminative conscience. We see how he is torn between killing Veasey, a preacher with shabby morals, or not (he doesn't), killing the bear cub or taking it home (he kills it). On one occasion, after helping a strange man, Junior, to rescue his bull, and being subsequently sold out by him to the Home Guard for the bounty, he comes back to take revenge on the informer.

Inman sees how easy it would be to do violence, and yet he is a fairminded young man, slow to anger even as he condemns the nastiness he sees around him. When Veasey is shot by the Home Guard, "Inman could find no great sorrow at his death, but neither could he find this an example of justice working its way around to show proof that the wrong a man does flies back at him." After he has killed Junior: "What lay before him was indeed a horrid thing, and yet Inman feared that the minds of all men share the same nature with little true variance." There is a bit of a latter-day Puritan in Inman here.

Even as he is being hunted on the river by men from the town, his thoughts take him far beyond his circumstances:

> He floated along thinking he would like to love the world as it was, and he felt a great deal of accomplishment for the occasions when he did, since the other was so easy. Hate took no effort other than to look about. It was a weakness, he acknowledged, to be of such a mind that all around him had to be fair for him to call it satisfactory.

Again he questions the ordering of the universe: "I wouldn't want to puzzle too long about the why of pain nor the frame of mind somebody would be in to make up a thing like it to begin with." Inman has experienced the rotten side of a world where Cain keeps on killing Abel, where rage explodes into viciousness and even the innocent are devastated. It is not surprising that his thoughts turn to metaphysical issues. He is no Elijah—an insignificant volunteer, not a major spokesman—but his mind and his actions are of a higher order than those militants he encounters wherever he goes. While Elijah might have agreed with General Lee's opinion in his own time, in today's world he would surely stand beside Inman.

Inman's death through the greater trickery of his enemy can be seen as bearing out his view of the world as a poor place with scarcely a hope for its recovery. As he believes, so it happens. Yet although war has brought out the dark side of many, it has not similarly corrupted Inman, though he fears it could do so. Others may deserve their fate, but he does not. There's no accounting. Here it is the gods of war who kill him, after letting him fight his crafty yet honourable way through the wilderness. He finds Ada, they have five tender days together, and he is finished.

One of the most haunting images is that of the crow. Although not a symbol, it is at least prescient. Ruby praises it for its willingness to accept whatever food comes its way. Inman admires crows for their ability to laugh at their enemies until they go away. The look of the hunched-over crow beside the creek causes Inman, who is ready to collapse, to get up off his hands and knees and walk again. At last, when he dies, he dreams of "a great number of crows, or at least the spirits of crows, dancing and singing in the upper limbs" of the blossoming trees. Perhaps the joke is on the gods after all.

While Inman is like Anna Jameson, an uprooted tree, afraid that he is dying at the core, there are three who survive in the wilderness by metaphorically or materially planting new trees. As Ada learns from Ruby the skills of farming, she also comes to understand and value the natural world. She comes to accept Ruby's view that you do certain tasks when the signs are right, never otherwise. The signs are for Ada "an expression of stewardship, a means of taking care, a discipline. They provided a ritual of concern for the patterns and tendencies of the material world where it might be seen to intersect with some other world." Ruby pays attention to the smallest details. "Each life with a story behind it. Every little gesture nature made to suggest a mind marking its life as its own caught Ruby's interest." As Ada eventually sees the finest particulars she recognizes that "every tiny place in the world seemed to make a home for some creature." The home that she shares with Ruby and eventually Ruby's husband and children, together with Stobrod and Ada's own daughter, is vaster than the homestead they occupy.

Throughout the novel runs a thin gleam of hope, a reaching for the eternal possibilities that have eluded Inman. The three chief survivors are the ones who exemplify hope, not only in their care for the natural world, but also in the way they live their lives—Ruby in her marriage, supporting hope with her "calm voice"; Ada with her painterly eye and her home that she shares with the others; Stobrod through music, which becomes a place where hope can be made manifest: "His playing was easy as a man drawing breath, yet with utter conviction in its centrality to a life worth claiming." Ada gives substance to this delicate hopefulness: "it seemed akin to miracle that Stobrod, of all people, should offer himself up as proof positive that no matter what a waste one has made of one's life, it is ever possible to find some path to redemption, however partial." Perhaps it isn't simply faint hope that makes me ask whether these three characters aren't the real heroes of this book, and Inman a good but floundering anti-hero, made wayless by war.

Frazier's world of plodding heroes, quiet victims, good souls, thoughtful seekers, foul murderers, and indifferent or bigoted citizens, despite its period setting, has a true twenty-first-century look to it. In some ways, like Inman, Frazier is a moderate, neither condemning nor praising this world outright, although he lacks Inman's elegiac notes. He does not hesitate to show us evil in its worst appearances, nor to allow it to be punished where the novel's circumstances permit. Yet where the little nuggets of loving-kindness appear, he makes them gleam in the midst of the foul river banks and tangled woods. All is not black and white: his heroes have weaknesses, and goodness comes from asocial people such as the gypsy folk. The uglies, however, who could have sprung from a Brechtian scenario, are as blatantly malevolent and superficial as Brecht's characters are. Because he has no obvious axe to grind, Frazier seems to me to have produced a fair-minded representation of our own present-day society: its grimness, its agonies, and its aspirations.

I have left till the end one episode that could almost be said to be the keynote, drawing together the goodness and evil that run through the novel, the pathos that is the final legacy of war. The incident has its own biblical model in the story of Hagar. Like Hagar's story, which is one small, separate segment of the narrative of Abraham's wanderings and eventual establishment in Canaan, the story of the young widow Sara shows the predicament of those abandoned by the masculine pursuits of genealogical security and war.

Hagar is the slave girl of Abraham and Sarah, who at that time were called Abram and Sarai, as they had not yet received their new names from God. When it seems that Sarah will be unable to bear children, she suggests to Abraham that he try to conceive a son with Hagar. As soon as she knows she is pregnant, Hagar begins lording it over Sarah, who then makes life so difficult for her that she runs out into the wilderness. God consoles her there, telling her she will have a son who will be named Ishmael. Hagar returns and has her child.

Some time later Sarah gives birth to Isaac. At Sarah's request, and with God's approval, Abraham gives Hagar and Ishmael bread and water and sends them out into the wilderness. As Hagar waits to die, she is once more consoled by the angel of God, who tells her Ishmael will be the ancestor of a great nation. Ishmael grows up and lives in the wilderness from then on.

When Inman finds Sara in her one-room cabin with her baby, she has lost just about everything she once had. Her husband has been killed in battle, and raiders have stolen her cow and burned down her barn. She has only a small plow with which to cultivate her pathetic little kitchen garden, and no friends to help. The sole means of keeping her from starving are her chickens and a sow, yet she takes in Inman, shelters and feeds him, and asks for nothing in return. Three Federal soldiers, after terrifying Sara by threatening to kill the baby, take away the sow and chickens. Inman kills all three soldiers, and brings back the animals. Following this success, he spends the second of two nights sleeping beside her in her bed, after sitting by the fire, "content and resting and happy." That is the only bright patch in the story, for Inman believes that with the hardships she will undergo she will be old before her time. Life in her wilderness will be right on the edge, and there are no promises of an enhanced future.

I am writing this in the midst of a wilderness that fulfills all my dreams of what a wilderness should be. This particular part of the Ontario lake country belongs to friends of ours; it is their refuge, their fantasy realized. Their beautifully simple cabin sits on a steep slope overlooking a rushing stream. Rocks thrust out into the water, either standing guard by the shore or acting as lips for the foamy white water heading south. Logs lie at the edge with their snouts in the water like recumbent crocodiles. On either side of the river are hundred-foot pines, trusty Scotch and glamorous white, thrusting their arms above the occasional slender birch. There are no boats, no waterskiers, no beach-partying visitors. We are the only humans within sight and sound. Our friends tell us that they have never seen a bear, even though many sightings have been reported in neighbouring districts.

This is the wilderness I always long for, and I'm sure I'm not alone, judging by the number of cars speeding north every weekend. In such a place one may imagine that all the nasty parts of the world have vanished, that the news doesn't exist, that you have all the time in the world to do just what you want to do, which may be simply to sit still and listen to the water. Deadlines, meetings, difficult decisions, cranky relatives, needy colleagues, importunate friends—all gone, for the time being. And the time being is what matters; lose it and we are lost.

In this wilderness I am safe, cared for by all the modern conveniences necessary, protected from the mosquitoes by screens, from the bears (I hope) by sturdy doors, from the cold by a woodstove, from the heat by a beautiful breeze. I can cook on a real stove, take a bath, chill my wine, listen to CDs.

All this is a far cry from the wilderness of nomadic peoples searching for a true home, or from that of the settlers in a country without decent roads, electricity, and indoor plumbing. This is not the wilderness that Hagar and Ishmael struggle to live in, nor the one where Sara must try to survive with her corn and her chickens. We are not refugees or even planters, but middle-class people affluent enough to take holidays, no less. The settings we love are those of the early settlers, but everything else is different now. Even if we try to recreate the rustic dwellings of our ancestors, we still do not go without our refrigerators and thick mattresses.

I am so glad we don't. I cannot see any great appeal in the pioneer way of life. For years we occupied an old family cottage, built in 1911. We had cold running water from the lake, and electricity had been installed just before we inherited it. This was living: three small children, an outhouse, no bath or shower, tin washtubs, and a rural turn-of-that-century kitchen. We adored it then; today I am glad we've moved on.

It does mean, though, that true wilderness for many people is not a drawing card. It is wilderness tamed and secured that we want. Most of us are neither mountaineers nor whitewater canoeists—today's true wilderness *voyageurs*. We are city folk who want to forget it for a while, to dream of a past or a future that is different from the daily round. To discover a way of being our "real" selves, whatever that means. Wilderness living is no hardship, really, even without hot water on tap. It is a joy, a life in hope, a heaven on earth. The Hebrews, Hagar and Ishmael, and Sara wouldn't understand us at all.

This wilderness we love is symbol, not geography. For example, at this cottage our car sits 100 metres away beside a paved road. We are 20 minutes from shops, where we can pick up the daily newspaper. We have a telephone; many people cannot survive a holiday in the north without their VCRs. We are avoiding the most entangling parts of our civilized lives by leaving these alone as much as possible. But they are there. We have made this wilderness into our dream land. On the other hand, if some homeless people decided to stay for a while on the banks of this river, they might find the bugs, the encroachment of animals on their food supplies, or the lack of enough blankets when the nights turn cool to be unpleasant and fearsome. The wilderness for them might be painful and ugly.

Having opened the door to the idea of the wilderness as a symbol, we can begin to look at the different sorts of environment and biography that are brought to bear on it and that change it drastically. This particular woodland place where I am sitting is invested with delight and yearning by some, but perhaps with discomfort and the desire to escape it by others, depending on who they are and why they are there. The physical characteristics are the same, but the emotive meaning changes. On the other hand, the symbol of the wilderness itself may change certain physical characteristics, while keeping its old meaning.

This wilderness that I am ecstatic about is one I have chosen to enter and to leave as I wish. Inman, on the other hand, has been forced to go through the wilderness in the hope of saving his life. Still, he has a home to go to, a goal to reach. This is not the wilderness of Hagar and Ishmael, or Sara. Their wilderness is a place they have been thrown into because there is no other place for them. Others, also outcasts, have been thrown into a wilderness of visually different aspect. We meet them in fiction as perhaps we never meet them in life.

John Berger's *King* is not a diatribe against society for allowing people to be homeless. It is a novel in all integrity, a brief episode in the life of a community of people living in a shantytown. In other words, we are not being conned by the author's simple, compelling prose into reading a political statement. What is there for us to learn is what we glean from any fine work of art, something that resonates with the sound of universal, timeless truth.

The narrator of the story is a dog, King. In case you are put off by this device, there is no cuteness to the mind or behaviour of this dog. Berger has probably chosen to tell the story this way because the dog is not like his other main characters, the homeless people, who are driven by circumstance into a narrow circle of self-absorption. King's way of life is that of a traveller and scavenger; he has already adapted, and is better able to protect and lead. He can wander and observe, carry news from one person to the other, alert the group to danger. He is both insider and outsider, and possibly the only one who could be the teller of the tale. He speaks to humans—those he wishes to talk to—as intelligibly as they to him.

The novel recounts one day and a night in the lives of a small group of people living in an empty city plot. I don't know whether Berger is alluding to the rules for Greek tragedy—that it should take place in one location on one day—when he sets his novel this way. Certainly the outcome of the story is grim, pathetic, sad, but it offers the reader no sense of satisfaction or emotional release, as we expect tragedy to do. It certainly does make me think about tragedy, and that may be what Berger intends.

During the day King introduces us to the members of the community one by one, brings us into more familiar acquaintance with the two people, Vica and Vico, with whom he lives in "The Hut," and gives us a tour of the land and the dwellings. This is truly a wasteland. It is located right beside a major highway. A building that stood there formerly was knocked down, becoming a scrap heap, and from then on the land has become a dump for old machinery and appliances and many unnameable bits and pieces. From this collection of junk, people have made homes. One person lives in a metal container, another in a concrete blockhouse; the rest do what they can with iron, plastic, and whatever else they can find. To get water, Vica and King fill jerrycans with water from the basins in the toilets at the gas station up the hill and push them back to The Hut in a stolen grocery cart. To support themselves, they steal flowers and vegetables from gardens and sell them in town. One of the members of the community, Marcello, has a Sunday job; another, Alfonso, sings in the subway. They steal from each other, have delusions and fights. They are no angels.

King tells us that to keep their spirits up, they think either about the future or the past:

> Every day the poor imagine their luck changing. They don't believe it will ever change, but they can't stop picturing to themselves what would happen if it did. And they don't want to miss the moment should it come.

When people here talk about the past, they tend to exaggerate, because sometimes the exaggerations, too, help to keep them a little warmer. As for the present, King sets it out as a kind of syllogism or equation:

Damp + cold = despair.
Despair + hunger = no god ever.
No god ever + alcohol = self-kill.

Two members of the community have killed themselves.

King calls whatever has brought all these people to this pass "the calamity." The world, he thinks, sees them as victims of a plague. "Deep down everybody knows that nobody is telling the truth about this plague. Nobody knows whom it selects and how. And so everywhere there is a fear of infection."

Vico and King have different views of the meaning of all this. King has decided, "If the world of men is vile and the rest so well made, there has to be a force for evil. Nothing else makes sense." Then, "If there's a force for evil, there has to be a force for good. No? And that means God, I said." However, "If everything was as beautiful as the forest, I'd never believe in him, I told them."

While King believes that God can help the poor, Vico sees his situation as hopeless.

There are places God doesn't come to.
The terrain?
No. Here. He points his finger like a gun at his own temple.

Vico believes matters can only continue to deteriorate. "Time passes, he is saying, and nine times out of ten time passing makes things worse!"

As it turns out, in this case he is right. After a fruitless day in town attempting to sell radishes, King arrives back at the shantytown ahead of Vico and Vica. It is 8:00 p.m. and dark. In the middle of the area is a jeep with a searchlight, four guards armed with submachine guns, and a bulldozer. The officer announces that this land is contaminated, so come out of your houses and we will relocate you in a better place. The bulldozer implies that whether they resist or not, their dwellings will be knocked down. This is what happens.

Two quotations from this scene immediately raise horrific memories of another such expulsion. The guard turns on the searchlight to sweep over the area. King says, "This sweeping was a sign. When it's dark everything is a sign. The guards wanted to show everybody who was hiding that they were going to be swept out." Then comes the announcement:

No reason for distress. We are asking you to come out, all of you. We are inviting you to a hot meal, like you don't often have. A hot meal. We are taking you to better accommodations. Transport is available.

This brings to mind the words quoted by Melvin Charney about the deportation of the Jews by the Nazis: "Better if they think they are going to a farm."[5] In this case, the doublespeak is what Vico calls "the second barbarism" that "kills a man and takes everything whilst it promises and talks of freedom." Rather than being a hated race, however, the homeless, Vico says, are society's mistake:

> A mistake, King, is hated more than an enemy. Mistakes don't surrender as enemies do. There's no such thing as a defeated mistake. Mistakes either exist or they don't, and if they do, they have to be covered over. We are their mistake, King. Never forget that.

Members of the group try feebly to protest, some by arguing, others by making an ineffectual bomb. Others close their eyes or convince themselves that no one will enter their squats to evict them. Out of this pathetic scene emerges Vico, hardly anyone's choice of a hero, with his face disfigured from a car crash, seen by the officer in charge as "the old derelict." He walks determinedly over to the officer, hiding a knife behind him, which he tries to thrust into the officer's belly. One kick by the officer lays him out on the ground, and the last King sees of him, a guard is standing over him, his machine gun pointed at his head.

Tear gas finally flushes them all out, and King leads them to a hollow in the ground where they can breathe. The bullhorn tells them that transport is waiting for them on the highway. Their situation is hopeless. "The guards would soon be searching. The bus was there to take them away and to separate them. Their eyes were burning. They waited because they did not know where to go."

The real reason for their evacuation is clear to King. It is "the last clumsy phase of an ill-organized operation for the flushing out of illegal squatters from land that had been bought for investment." Contaminated soil be damned. Ditto better accommodation.

King, who has been their helper and mainstay all along, now in his dog's mind sees himself as the leader of a group of people transformed into dogs, whom he draws towards the river and the freedom of the fields beyond. As he reaches the bridge, he turns around, and sees no one following. They are still waiting in the hollow, future unknown. King's last thoughts are about his beloved Vica, in whose arms he loved to lie.

This is the first time that I have read a novel about today's invisible people—neither wicked nor stigmatized, neither cruel nor callous, but people like us, the difference being that they are society's "mistake." In a sense they are the corporate version of Willy Loman in *Death of a Salesman*, neither evil nor noble, with only a turn of fortune or accident separating us from them. Vico, if he can be believed, was an inventor in charge of a factory; Vica took singing lessons in Zürich. There but for—what?—go we. Yet they are ignored, tossed away, and we go on regardless. Just as Zola's *Germinal* cannot help but turn our minds to the frightful treatment of miners in northern France, and Dickens, though writing lively fiction, directs us to the horrible effects of nineteenth-century industrialization on human lives, so *King* has an urgency for the twenty-first century that goes beyond the novelist's task of spinning a meaningful tale. In twenty or thirty years, perhaps, we hope that the imperative to correct our "mistake" will have changed society so much that the book will be read as an important work of fiction, no more. For now, the political demand to open our eyes speaks through a book that presents with clear-sighted sympathy the grandeur of the human spirit wherever it is housed.

Inman and Vico: both little men, ordinary people, like us, but they are truth-tellers with a sterling gleam of integrity and courage that emerges when the need is great, and sets them above you and me in our pantheon of heroes. In such a world as we have today, where greatness is rarely found, where even when it does seem to exist it turns out to be flawed or deceiving, they are possibly the best we can hope for. I suppose that's not such a bad thing to want.

In both *Cold Mountain* and *King*, the metaphysical and moral foundations of good old-time religion are urgently questioned. There seems to be a lack of connection between the origin of good and evil and those human lives that are "mistakes." Inman fears that his life, now blotted by the war, may be written off as a "dark mistake." Both novels see a contrast between the natural world and the vileness of men's behaviour. Both question the activity of God to set things right. While Vico thinks that God does not have control of what happens to his mind (and soul?), Inman thinks God does not even keep the world going "in right order." He questions the need for pain in the world, the cruelty that cannot be called divine justice. As for the "mistakes," neither novel looks to God for explanation or cure. God does not bear either the responsibility or the ability to help. The old divinity seems here to be referred to only as a courtesy, a memory that is soon to slip away. The world as the heroes of these books see it will soon lose track of God altogether.

It's rather late in the game—although fine for Inman, a character set in the nineteenth century—to be disputing the origin of evil, an impossible argument if one insists upon divine omnipotence, another term that is past its prime. The real issue today is not who's responsible for evil, God or his adversaries, but who on earth carries it out, and how can we stop it? Letting go of this old line of thought, however, means dropping a lot more than a piece of illicit logic. It means withdrawing from a whole universe of meaning, walking away from a brilliant imperial court with its panoply of colour, chant, and ceremony. It means leaving a high, holy place that is or was home.

There's the rub. I really want all the perks of the old kingdom without the responsibility of having to subscribe to its ordinances or give allegiance to its beliefs. I may want to leave this old circumscribed place I call home, but I'm not going without my wardrobe, my CDs, and the grand piano.

My beloved old liturgical home was England. I loved the Anglican liturgy, with its hymns, chants, anthems, and all. I loved the singing of the English choir schools. Too disembodied, said my friend Ernie, himself a product of this environment and a theologian. I disagreed: it was heaven on earth. (How is it that, so many years later, I have to admit that my friends are right? This happens far too often to be ignored.) I still love Kings' College Choir and its ilk, but as my theological centre has caved in, so my liturgical delight has dimmed. These days my musical centre is, as it has been for years, wherever that old Kapellmeister of the Thomaskirche, J.S. himself, is playing; it is with Messaien in full flight; it dreams in Romanesque basilicas with César Franck and Marcel Dupré. Musically I'm not lost; liturgically I am beginning to wander.

The reason, of course, is that the theology of today doesn't fit the liturgical performance. Over the last 40 years or so I've tramped back and forth along many of the new paths that were opened up by what was called at the beginning the "New Theology." I read and tried to think about the ideas coming from the Cambridge group and from the American secularists, Harvey Cox et al. I finally came back to Paul Tillich, and there I stayed, and still do to a certain extent. Although the thought of these writers clearly put holes in the canvas of the old mythological universe, it wasn't enough to break it up completely. I could have my liturgical painting almost intact, without going through great cognitive dissonance about what it all meant.

With the growth in depth and wisdom of feminist theology today, I have moved on. For me it is—some of it—the liveliest, most compassionate and morally sound thought about the Christian enterprise today. It is only just beginning to shake off its hostile anti-world stance of its early days, and to set out to engage that world through its exuberant, compelling arguments. I haven't taken a position on this theological horizon. I'm not capable of arriving at one on my own, and in fact one of the main points of this group of feminist thinkers is that no one goes it on her own today. Theology is world-focussed, not self-centred. What I do know is that it goes completely against the world picture engendered by classical theology, or that version that the churches allude to today. This means that old-time liturgy that expressed and enhanced that world picture is completely out of sync with the best of contemporary Christian thought; in fact, it is opposed to it, severely.

So here I am, finally at an impasse. Writing this book has forced me to declare myself. My beautiful old home is a foreign place now. I certainly can't go home again. Where shall I look for another? Pillar of fire, where are you? Reassuring cloud by day?

4

— AFTER THE HOLOCAUST —

What else are the lives but a journey to the vacant
Satisfaction of death? And the mask
They wear tonight through their waste
Is death's rehearsal. For I too shall escape,
We read in the faces; and what is there we possessed
That we were unwilling to trade for this?

Randall Jarrell, "The Refugees"

The Christian, as much as the Jew, is still on the way through the desert between the
Exodus and the Promised Land, with many a golden idol and broken tablet along the
way.

Rosemary Radford Ruether, *Faith and Fratricide*

My life is darker than night and deeper than hell.

Henry Kreisel, *The Betrayal*

T he first time I ever came to realize what was meant by a ghetto was on a trip to Prague about a dozen years ago. This was in the earliest days of its most recent emancipation, when there were practically no hotels, no bank machines or Kodak films to be had, the taxi drivers weren't robbers, and the city had barely begun the prettification that has turned it into the capital of charm today. Even then in its grubby state it was an astonishing place, with its *art nouveau* architecture, the faded palaces and townhouses clasped with lingering distinction to the steep cobbled streets (Kafka's *The Castle* hadn't been filmed yet). Obviously it had been a most graceful, cultivated city. The historic centre isn't large, there was plenty of time to explore, and so we found ourselves going beyond the Old Town into the former Jewish quarter.

Several synagogues were in the process of restoration at that time, and one was certainly in use, the only one we weren't allowed to enter. The others have become museums of Jewish art, or memorials. Beside one ancient synagogue is the old Jewish cemetery, so old that it has been closed to burials since the eighteenth century. The land it occupies is about the size of a small backyard. It is said to hold the remains of 20,000 Jews. This was all the land the Jews were allowed by the city for their burials, and so they had to bury people in layers, about a dozen of them.

Another small building, which had just recently been reopened to the public, was the Pinkas synagogue. After the war it was designated as the site of a memorial to the over 77,000 Czech Jews who were killed in the Holocaust. Their names were all inscribed on the walls inside. Then the Russians closed it, for restoration work, it was said. When they left town it was discovered that dampness had obliterated almost all the names. No restoration work had taken place. When we saw it, the walls had been freshly whitewashed, and the task of rewriting the names had begun. Donations were being requested to help complete the work. It seemed that the Russians had been attempting metaphorically what the Nazis had tried to do in actuality. The loss of a name is a total erasure of the person, the worst loss of all.

In writing about people who, like Hagar, and Elijah, and even Moses, were thrown out into the wilderness because there was no other place to go, I find it impossible not to consider the fate of their direct descendants, the Jews of Europe during the period that began in the 1930s in Germany and reached its cataclysmic state during World War II. It would be a travesty, and a cruel diminishment of the fact of the *univers concentrationnaire*, to say that the Jews who were caught up in it and murdered were in a wilderness. The closest imagery one can use to describe this experience is that of the medieval visions of hell. Hell—neither this kind nor any other—is not something I wish to talk about. Others who have real knowledge of the Holocaust have done so, painfully and honourably. I cannot imagine it and would not presume.

I do want to ask, however, what the world must be like for those who survived the horrors of Auschwitz, or who escaped them, only to discover later what had taken place. I have a friend who lived with his family in the forests of southern France for over a year. When the war ended, he, a boy of 12, found out about the effects of the Holocaust. He learned that his uncle and aunt, together with 34 other Jews, had been thrown alive down a well, their bodies covered with bags of cement and stones: this was to repay the local people for the *résistants'* killing of some German soldiers. It was impossible to know what effect this discovery had upon this outwardly gentle man, who took up sculpture in order to sublimate these memories, he said.

Others, notably Elie Wiesel and Primo Levi, who were interned in two of the death camps and survived, have used their writing to defuse the ghastliness of the memory and to make sure that the story is told for future generations. Although they have written diaries and autobiographies, we can never know what singular wildernesses they have been living in since the war ended. The bleakness and severity of these exceeds my imagination.

I had just entered my teens when the war ended, and I remember people talking a great deal about the "displaced persons" (DPs) who were coming to Canada from Europe. (The term "New Canadian" hadn't been invented yet, and anyway it wouldn't have applied at this stage.) I can't recall ever meeting any of them then, but I have kept the impression that they were somewhat looked down upon for having been displaced, almost as though every decent person should have a home, or certainly know where it once was. I decided that they were pathetic people, and probably not very capable. As the stories came out, I learned that many of them were professionals, that some had formerly held great possessions, but that the war had destroyed all their property and separated them from their families. I do not know how many of these DPs were Jews.

About ten years after the war, I was introduced to a lively intellectual group of former Europeans, mostly Jews who had emigrated just before Hitler sealed off the borders and began herding people into camps for deportation. Others in this group of friends had stayed in Europe but escaped persecution. Although we met often for dinner, concerts, films, and conversation, it never even occurred to me to ask any of them their stories, where they came from, and how they had escaped. Although we had all been children during that period, I didn't stop to wonder whether their parents were still alive or had perished. The best I managed to do was to "understand" when one friend, a Czech, declined to go to a concert by the Berlin Philharmonic, whose conductor, Herbert von Karajan, had been reviled as a Nazi sympathizer. I of course attended, as did some others in the group.

Whether they were Jewish or Romany, or simply homeless on account of the war, these uprooted people entered a world that, after the celebrations and parades and fireworks had subsided in 1945, would have been grimly strange. There is no such thing as a fresh start: the burden of memory and loss is not one you can lay down by wishful thinking or determination. The wilderness for those with such burdens is more internal than external, the losses irreplaceable. To give an image to this inscape has been the work of some writers. To give it meaning and an adequate response is the even more difficult task of others.

All Western literature since the 1940s is post-Holocaust literature, whether the writers are conscious of it or not. Many social upheavals marked the twentieth century, many revolutionary discoveries changed our way of thinking, and the world witnessed many horrors and disasters both natural and unnatural. Yet there has been nothing like the Holocaust, which encompasses all of these. Since the utterly despicable activity of the Nazis and their collaborators towards the Jews, the gypsies and others deemed unfit to live, there have been ferocious attempts at genocide. There has never been, before or since, a consciously determined, rationally planned, systematic effort, thoroughly researched with experimentation on live models, to eradicate a group of people simply because they existed. And the ideas and procedures for this program came out of the Western culture and society that we all inherited and share. We think and write in the face of this fact, or not, as we choose. But it is there.

Our wilderness—for if you do not find yourself joined in doubt and sorrow with those whose suffering and indignity were unthinkable before this time, then stop reading now—is not physical. Perhaps it is even less emotional than it is intellectual and spiritual, especially the latter. The Holocaust has shocked and upset our beliefs in liberalism, enlightenment, the morality of our culture, and the divine underpinnings to that culture that have held everything in place. As Simon Sibelman writes, "As in a crystal, Auschwitz stands as the focal point through which all facets of contemporary civilization and culture pass."[6] True, it hasn't upset everyone. Some fundamentalist groups among both Christians and Jews still believe nothing has changed. And plenty of people have denied that such a thing could have happened, or if it did, that they and theirs were certainly not responsible; they didn't know anything about it. To others—and I wish I could say most of us—the Holocaust has made such a difference to our thinking about God and about human behaviour that the world will never be seen in the same way again.

There are many examples of the "literature of atrocity,"[7] as Lawrence Langer calls it, in which writers, often survivors, have attempted in literary or biographical form to tell the story of the unutterable so that we may never forget. I have found fewer works in which the wilderness of the aftermath has been pictured.

The great novelist who is associated with the Holocaust is Elie Wiesel, himself a concentration camp survivor. The books he has written as fiction are transparently autobiographical, and show the writer himself emerging gradually from the black hole of his wartime experience into a bizarre new world at the age of 16. Each novel brings him a step further in creating a different life for himself. So, three novels after *Night*, which was set in Büchenwald, comes *The Gates of the Forest* (*Les portes de la forêt*) in 1964.

The novel is divided into four sections, each given a season title. It begins in spring to tell the story of a young man of 17, Gregor, who escapes from a Hungarian ghetto with his father just as the deportations are beginning. Leaving him in a cave, his father goes out, promising to return in three days. He never comes back. Gregor finds shelter first in the forest, then in the village home of an old family servant, and finally in another part of the forest with a group of Jewish partisans. His forced wanderings end, at least physically, some years later in New York.

Gregor, the homeless sole survivor of his family, is befriended and mentored, often in mysterious ways, by an unusual collection of heroes. There is Gavriel, who arrives at the cave one day with knowledge of the destruction of the ghetto and deportation of the Jews. Until that moment believed he was the only Jew alive. When the police bring the dogs out to hunt through the forest for the one whom they also believe is the last Jew alive, Gavriel gives himself up to save Gregor.

Maria, the family retainer, takes Gregor in, and introduces him to the village as the mute and probably deaf son of her wayward sister Ileana. In what is the most dramatic scene of the novel, Gregor is attacked by the villagers, and rescued at the last minute by the village's secretive nobleman, Count Petruskanu. In the forest where Petruskanu leaves him, the suspicious partisans bring him to their leader, who turns out to be his childhood protector, Leib the Lion. Leib, as courageous as ever, arranges a mission to the prison to rescue Gavriel who, Gregor believes, is inside. The mission backfires, and Leib is captured.

In the last section of the book, "Winter," Gregor is now living in New York, married to Leib's beloved Clara, who cannot rid herself of his memory, and wants to turn Gregor into another Leib. Gregor learns from two men, the Rebbe and a stranger, how to begin to resolve his life, even if none of the questions that plague him are answered.

The forest is a strange and ambiguous wilderness in this novel. Its characteristics are a reflection of Gregor's conflicting emotions at different stages of his journeying. In his first period of hiding, alone for the first time, the forest makes him feel secure, yet at the same time he is constantly on the alert for threatening sounds: "At times it seemed to him as if the forest were filled with nocturnal hunters, each one of them like the Angel of Death, with a thousand eyes to strangle man's voice and to deform his body." The sound of footsteps coming through the forest, which turn out to be Gavriel's, causes him to panic and cry out. His security is fragile at best. I recall that Simon Schama says that some Polish Jews got out of the ghetto and hid without discovery in the Lithuanian forests, but many others were taken into the forest by the SS and shot there. No wonder the forest has ambivalent overtones for Wiesel.

In his second period of hiding in the forest, Gregor thinks of it again as a secure place, but also as one that holds him captive: "We are prisoners of this forest which, like a living being, holds its breath and curious, advances, leaning forward, on the alert, so as not to lose the least rustle, the least whisper." The forest listens and remembers everything. The partisans are prisoners of the forest, because outside it "the earth and sky of Europe had become great, haunted cemeteries." They have nowhere to go. Gregor says it's the end of the world.

By the end of the novel, Gregor, who is thinking of leaving Clara because she will not relinquish her obsession with the memory of Leib, recalls the listening forest as a place of freedom and simplicity. "The forest meditates: it listens to voices instead of stifling them." In it, he thinks, "I am what I choose to be....There is no divorce between self and its image, between being and acting. I am the act, the image, one and indivisible." It sounds like an experience one of the prophets might have had in the wilderness.

The forest, rather than simply expressing Gregor's emotions at the time, has grown into a somewhat amorphous symbol. It transcends itself, but vaguely, just as does the image Wiesel paints of the clouds as Jews returning to light their home fires. Right from the start this forest extends far beyond trees and caves: "There was no use running away from this forest, it is everywhere, separating man from the image of his destiny and from the death of this destiny." I don't know whether this idea is more confusing in the English translation, or whether Wiesel is so overwhelmed by his own thought that it remains ambiguous. (I do get the impression, even in the translation, of a book written through overpowering emotions.) It is nevertheless a symbol of great power in the novel, for here it is again when Gregor and Leib are walking through the forest together:

> The saint and the solitary...come here not only to purify their bodies and their passions, but also to listen and tremble, to tremble as they listen to this roaring voice which, before creation, before the liberation of the word, already contained form and matter, joy and defeat, and that which separates and reconciles them, from all of which the universe, time, and their own secret life were fashioned.

The forest may be the voice, or the place where the voice is heard, just as Elijah experienced it; in either case the meaning is immense.

For all that Wiesel brings out the forest in its mysterious power, it remains primarily the locus for important conversations and events, and the occasion for Gregor to question, act, and question again. Its power recedes against the strength of the theme, and although it seems to be related to this theme, it is difficult to put together any argument about it in linear form. The novel is not an argument; it is a series of fragments that gives glimpses of a life strained to the utmost.

The book's emotional heartland is the cry of anguish that transposes itself into questions crucial to the lives of the characters (and by extension, to our own lives): What is a human being now? Has the Messiah arrived, or is he coming? What shall we do now?

In the two most devastating episodes in the novel, young Gregor discovers himself involved unwittingly and unwillingly in actions that reveal something of human nature to which he was naively oblivious before. As Maria's pretend mute nephew, Gregor becomes the village pet. He is welcomed everywhere and learns all the shabby and licentious secrets of the villagers, who know that he is more to be trusted with them than is the priest. Many of the men have had relations, successful or not, with Ileana, his supposed mother. Then the schoolmaster decides to put on a play about Judas, and, since none of the students is willing to take this part, Maria very reluctantly agrees to let Gregor do so. Near the end of the play Judas comes onstage, and to all the dramatized anger of the children is added that of the adults in the audience. First it is turned against the Jews whom Judas represents, and then against Gregor himself for being the son of the woman who made fools of many of them. Words become blows, until finally Gregor speaks. This stops everything, as the villagers fall to the ground, believing a miracle has taken place. Gregor tells them who he really is, and, as they realize that he knows all their secrets, their anger propels the worst attack of all. At the point when his life seems to be in danger, the count whisks him away to join the partisans.

This is what Gregor learns:

The peasants had surged to their feet. Their nostrils were quivering and they shouted at the top of their lungs, with their wives echoing them. They were a mob, and the mob wanted blood....

Only yesterday these people had talked to him, gripped his arm, offered him an apple, a cluster of raisins, a kindly word.... They haven't changed, Gregor said to himself without bitterness, and I haven't changed either. We have remained what we were, neither more nor less, and yet in the farthest corner of their being, and of mine too, something has been transfigured. Conditions are no longer the same.

It is a strange use of the word "transfigured," but clearly Gregor has come to look at humanness in an entirely different light.

In the second episode Gregor learns another profoundly disturbing lesson. When he tells Leib the Lion, who now leads the partisans, that he thinks the strange, heroic Gavriel is in prison, Leib decides that they must rescue him. He sets up a scheme by which Gregor and Clara will socialize with one of the prison guards and try to learn whether Gavriel is there, and how to find him. Leib will rendezvous with them later in the town. Unfortunately, the guard, knowing that they are looking for a Jew, alerts the other guards, who catch Leib. Gavriel is nowhere to be seen, and Leib is deported. Gregor learns that even those who try to do good may do as much evil as those with ill intent. "Now Gregor understood everything, both his own guilt and that of his audience [the partisans]. The injustice perpetrated in an unknown land concerns me; I am responsible. He who is not among the victims is with the executioners."

Although this last sentence rings with authority at a critical point in the novel, it is not the final word. Gregor carries his guilt for being an ignorant executioner with him after the war to America, but he is finally ready to say to Clara that one must not be seduced by one's ghosts: "they'll continue to haunt us, but we must fight them. It will be a bitter, austere, obstinate battle. The struggle to survive will begin here, in this room, where we are sitting."

Throughout this time of isolation and fear, Gregor looks to older, wiser men to make sense of what is happening. First to enter his life is the mysterious Gavriel. He arrives out of nowhere, claiming that he has lost his name. Gregor gives him his own Jewish name, Gavriel, which means angel of God. Is Gavriel in fact such a being? His conversation seems to suggest some supernatural power: "As I walk through this world," he says, "I find empty cities...." What Jew could escape detection like this? Then, when he is ready to give himself up to the soldiers, he says, "They can't do anything to me. How often must I tell you that?" Even if it were untrue, Gavriel is a person who is larger than life. At one point Gregor suspects that Gavriel was an illusion he had, yet "[h]e admits that, had it not been for his apparent meeting with Gavriel, and he insisted on *apparent*, he would not have been able to endure and his being would not have been revealed to him." Later on, Gregor identifies Gavriel with Count Petruskanu and, in New York, with a stranger who comes to a Hasidic celebration, but afterwards he realizes that neither is Gavriel. Wiesel himself, when asked who is Gavriel, gave an ambiguous answer: "In the end, it is up to Gavriel to identify himself. If he chooses to say nothing, Gregor could perhaps explain for him."[8]

Gavriel is the one who first asks the question about the Messiah. He tells Gregor that he asked Elijah when the Messiah will come, because God has chosen Elijah to make the announcement of the Messiah's arrival to the people. Gavriel tells Elijah, "If the Messiah doesn't hurry, he may be too late; there will be no one left to save." Elijah replies,

> He's not coming because he has already come.... The Messiah is everywhere. Ever present, he gives each passing moment its taste of drunkenness, desolation, and ashes. He has a name, a face, and a destiny. On the day when his name and face and destiny are one, all masks will fall, time will be freed of its chains, and he will link it to God, as he will link to God drunkenness and desolation and ashes.

He tells Gavriel that even God does not know when that day will come.

Gavriel thinks he has found the Messiah in Moshe, the synagogue's beadle. After vainly trying to persuade him to save his people, Gavriel has decided that the Messiah has become corrupted by being among people too long. "The Messiah came," he says, "and nothing changed.... The Messiah came, and the executioner goes right on executing. The Messiah came and the world is a vast slaughterhouse, as it was before."

Gregor begins to think that the Messiah is not one saviour, but every man led to the slaughter:

> And hundreds of hearts ceased beating, ceased advancing toward a future at the end of which a Messiah—it didn't matter who—was supposed to receive them. "Fire!" called out the officers, and the Messiah himself, a thousand times, a thousand, thousand times multiplied, fell into the ditch.

Rather confusingly, Gregor tells Leib that the Messiah is not coming: "he got lost along the way, and from now on the clouds will obscure his sight." And at the same time, he agrees with Gavriel that "the Messiah has come too late, that he's killed anew every day by men and by God. God, too, is killed every day. Who'll dare speak tomorrow of divine grace and mercy or of man as a savior?"

In his final affirmation at the end of the book, Gregor seems to be saying that there is no one hero to come and save; people are their own hope and strength.

> Whether or not the Messiah comes doesn't matter; we'll manage without him. It is because it is too late that we are commanded to hope. We shall be honest and humble and strong, and then he will come, he will come every day, thousands of times every day. He will have no face, because he will have a thousand faces. The Messiah isn't one man, Clara, he's all men. As long as there are men there will be a Messiah.

The Gates of the Forest is a dark book, filled with the grim beasts of fear—of betrayal, of capture, of not knowing. Because it is not a treatise but a novel, there's a forceful kind of realism in the lack of consistency to the questions and the answers about where the human race is headed, and who, if anyone, is to lead and save. Despite the hero's experiences, which we have been told run very close to the author's, the book ends with the above declaration, a hope against hope. It may be only a pinpoint in the dark, but it is a light.

This book is a fiction, the experiences behind it not so. Wiesel, who saw his father die in Büchenwald just before the war ended, is a survivor who has chosen to write out his anguish, to speak in order to remind the world so that such a horror never happens again. Primo Levi, who was in Auschwitz and Büchenwald for a year, tries to describe, in *The Drowned and the Saved*, what it felt like for those who emerged from the camps.

> In the majority of cases, the hour of liberation was neither joyful nor lighthearted. For most it occurred against a tragic background of destruction, slaughter, and suffering. Just as they felt they were again becoming men, that is, responsible, the sorrows of men returned: the sorrow of the dispersed or lost family; the universal suffering all around; their own exhaustion, which seemed definitive, past cure; the problems of a life to begin all over again amid the rubble, often alone.[9]

George Steiner, whose family had left Vienna for Paris in the 1920s, is one of the most thoughtful and incisive inquirers into the devastating effects of the Holocaust on Western culture, and into the ways by which our culture actually produced the Holocaust. He draws attention to the roots of anti-Semitism in Christian theology, and argues that Christians have from earliest times been outraged at the unwillingness of Jews to accept Jesus as the Messiah. Building on this ancient attitude, the Nazis added their own peculiar hatreds bolstered by untenable racial myths. Here is how the Nazis came to see the Jew:

> He was to be recognized as a being less than human. Torture and fear were to reduce him to a subhuman status. In the fantastications of Nazism, those starved, beaten, gassed to extinction were not men and women and children but vermin, members of a species other than that of man.[10]

Even a scant knowledge of this process of dehumanization makes it seem remarkable that survivors were left with any sense of identity at all, as humans with a life ahead, let alone as the lonely, probably lone, members of a family, homeless and stateless. They could hardly return to a town or village whose other citizens had rejected or betrayed them. It is no wonder that there were many suicides. After living for many years in this post-Shoah wilderness, the memory of that time was all or part of the cause of Levi's suicide in 1987, and of the psychologist Bruno Bettelheim's in 1990.

In 2002, a novel came out that describes vividly the state of mind and behaviour of a woman who has just emerged from a concentration camp. *Le Non de Klara* is the first novel of Soazig Aaron, but because it has only appeared in French, I won't give it the attention it deserves as the winner of the 2002 Prix Goncourt for a first novel. Speculation about the author, about whom little is known, has already commenced: was this a story based on first-hand experience, or is it a singular piece of fiction? The answer does not matter to the reader. The novel's great strength is the portrait of Klara, the fictional heroine, as drawn in a journal kept by her sister-in-law. We see how she comes to view the worlds she has experienced within and outside the concentration camp, and how the former affects the latter.

Klara, who is German, has come to a refugee centre in Paris, where her sister-in-law Angélika lives with her doctor husband. On meeting her sister she announces that she is going to leave for America, and that she does not wish to see her three-year-old daughter, Victoire, who has been cared for by Angélika. Klara's husband has been shot as a resistance fighter.

When Angélika brings her home from the refugee centre, she says that Klara has "a kind of madness about her." She paces the room and smokes constantly, or pounds the pillow on the couch. Her voice, a monotone, is hoarse. Angélika realizes that she mustn't embrace her: her body says, "Don't touch me." Her eyes are vacant, deep, and cold; Angélika has seen many return from the camps with eyes like Klara's. Klara cannot sleep, except for a few minutes at a time, and when she does she has nightmares. She says that she had no nightmares in Auschwitz; it *was* the nightmare.

When she begins to talk about her experiences, she spills it all out, sparing no horrible details. She begins by saying that she will never speak German again, because *they* have ruined it. Even the camp she refers to by its real Polish name, Oswiecim, although mainly she just calls it *"là-bas"* (over there). She feels as if her shadow remains *"là-bas,"* and she talks of the smoke and smell there. Our knowledge of extremes is of no help; the extremity of what happened there cannot be transmitted. Her friends died there, and she has no more tears to tell about them. She has "nostalgia for tears." She wants no more friends.

As her voice gradually begins to take on variations of tone, Angélika reports a change from the non-feeling state to one of anger and violence, although Klara describes her hatred "coolly, almost lightly." Her anger helped her to live; by saying no to everything, she survived.

Klara's "no" is addressed to all the ideals and characteristics that give one an identity. She says no to being Jewish; although she comes from a Jewish line, she is not religious, and she sees herself as being German. If she were to accept the designation of being Jewish, she would be giving in to Hitler. She refuses to be racist. She has given up her country and her own language. She has said no to her daughter, because she knows herself to be dead inside, and may perhaps never recover. She does not wish to give her daughter that sort of future.

God, she says, is burning in Oswiecim, and all philosophies have gone up in smoke: "The only thing one could say for certain is that the human being is "despicably stubborn." Pardon has no meaning, but neither has revenge. The only real, good part of life that is left, in bits and pieces, is poetry.

Klara's farewell to Angélika shows a trace of the old Klara, full of kindly understanding. This little scene, and her praise of poetry, are the only signs that a life may be possible for her, somewhere, sometime. The novelist puts no emphasis on this; in fact, the ending of the book, in which Klara abruptly kills two vile former neighbours in Berlin, does nothing to alleviate the bitter hopelessness of the whole story. As the narrative proceeds, Klara's relatives begin to understand why this is so, and so do we.

Writing in 1986, Primo Levi was well aware of the tricks that memory can play, just in the ordinary course of living, when it comes to remembering something traumatic. In the post-Holocaust situation, the victims find it too painful to remember, and so the worst is mercifully buried. The torturers may begin to falsify the truth consciously for fear of opprobrium, shame, or even guilt; gradually over time

> ... the distinction between true and false progressively loses its contours, and man ends by fully believing the story he has told so many times and continues to tell, polishing and retouching here and there the details which are least credible or incongruous or incompatible with the acquired picture of historically accepted events.... [11]

Then there were all the others: those who lived in Germany and who for the most part would have known something of what was going on. Steiner gives examples to show that people did certainly know what was happening and says, "Men are accomplices to that which leaves them indifferent."[12]

How did the indifferent treat the past? Erna Paris, investigating the lies people tell about atrocities executed in different countries, gives a contemporary example. A couple of artists with a hidden microphone question people in a formerly Jewish Berlin neighbourhood:

> "Do you know what group of people used to live here?" they asked an elderly lady of about eighty who was out walking her poodles.
>
> "I think they were Jewish citizens," she replied.
>
> "Do you know where they are now?" asked the artists.
>
> The woman thought for a moment. "Well, they are not here. I think they left for Israel," she said.
>
> "Did you know about the deportations?"

"There *were* no deportations here," the woman stated firmly. "They all survived and now they live in Israel."[13]

Paris describes three major lies that the French swallowed instead of accepting the far more damning truths about their wartime behaviour. There was the belief stemming from de Gaulle that the "real" government of France was in England and that France had therefore won the war with the Allies. It was better for the country to believe this than to deal with all the people who had collaborated with the Germans. Following from this was the belief that everyone had been part of the Resistance, when in fact only 1 per cent of the population had been *résistants*. The third lie was that people either did not know where the Jews were being sent (those in charge said this), or did not know about the deportations at all. As Paris says, "France, it turned out, was the only occupied Western European country to have enacted its own anti-Jewish legislation. Thanks to the willing assistance of the French, the Germans had needed only twenty-five hundred Gestapo police for the entire occupied territory."[14]

Finally, there are all of us, with our sanitized memories. But that will have to wait until later in this chapter.

Steiner speaks of the "creative amnesia" that lies behind the destruction of many World War II sites, and the rebuilding afresh. "It was indecent to survive," he says, "let alone prosper again, in the graphic presence of the immediate past."[15] These words were written in 1971; more recently, however, Paris has visited sites that do refer, euphemistically or otherwise, to the Holocaust. Architect Melvin Charney, asked to submit a proposal to the international art exhibition *Documenta* 7 in 1981, planned to reconstruct the façade of the railway entrance to Auschwitz-Birkenau—an ordinary-seeming building intended to deceive everyone as to its inner workings—across from the present railway station in Darmstadt. He says,

> There were objections to this project. Drawings of the installation were removed from an exhibition of proposals for *Documenta Urbana*. The invocation of its image seemed to undermine both the feigned silence of postwar modernism and of cultural practices in general.[16]

It cannot be easy to live with lies and deceptions as crucial as these, which define who you are as a human being, even if at some level of your mind you have come to believe they are the truth. Paris says that families did not tell their children about their participation in the war, and now when asked about it, they have refused to say anything. The second generation, however, is discovering that what it believed to be true about the past is nothing like what really happened. For these descendants to find that their history is a lie is to be thrown into a devastating wilderness of dense fog and unsafe footing, a place they cannot abide. They have begun to demand and pronounce the truth. Tombstones of Jews in Père Lachaise cemetery in Paris have been altered from the euphemistic and untrue "Mort pour la France" (died for France) to "Murdered at Auschwitz." Two questions haunt them: What do we do about the past? And what does it mean for the future?

These questions are an important part of the fabric of German writer and lawyer Bernhard Schlink's novel *The Reader* (*Der Vorleser*), which originally appeared in Germany in 1995, 50 years after the end of World War II, and in English translation in 1997. The novel is set in three time periods: the 1950s, 1960s, and 1980s. It is the story of a 15-year-old boy who falls in love for the first time with Hanna, a woman of 36. Besides discovering her passion for washing her young lover, being read to, and making love, Michael learns nothing about her past. After an affair of several months, Hanna disappears one day without warning. Some years later Michael, now a law student, discovers Hanna on trial for her actions as an SS guard, the most horrific of which was allowing several hundred Jewish women to burn to death inside a locked church that had been ignited by a bomb. After much badgering and many accusations by the other defendants, Hanna admits that she wrote a false report of the deed and is sentenced to life imprisonment; the others receive lighter sentences for their part in the action. Just before the trial ends, Michael realizes that Hanna can neither read nor write, and she is so ashamed to admit this that she decides to confess to something she did not do rather than expose her ignorance. (She admits that she and the others didn't unlock the church and let the women out because they were afraid they would lose control of their prisoners.) He goes to tell the trial judge, but then departs without saying anything. After 18 years in prison, during which time Michael sends her tapes of books he reads to her and she eventually learns to read and write, Hanna is granted release. The night before Michael is to collect her, she hangs herself.

The touchstones to this novel are the ambivalence of feelings on the part of the hero and the moral uncertainties raised by both Michael and Hanna. To begin with, the emotional roller coaster is one that any teenager might ride: Michael lurches between feelings of extreme self-confidence and the lack of it. He loves Hanna, but she has the ability to make him think he's in the wrong and needs to apologize guiltily for his behaviour. Eventually his feelings wane somewhat, they have fights, and although he apologizes, still he is "filled with resentment." He accuses himself of betraying her by never telling his school friends about her. The last time they make love is ominous: "She also gave herself in a way she had never done before. She didn't abandon all reserve, she never did that. But it was as if she wanted us to drown together." After she disappears, Michael determines "[n]ever to let myself be humiliated or humiliate myself after Hanna, never to take guilt upon myself or feel guilty, never again to love anyone whom it would hurt to lose...." At the same time, he says, "I adopted a posture of arrogant superiority. I behaved as if nothing could touch or shake or confuse me.... This juxtaposition of callousness and extreme sensitivity seemed suspicious even to me."

Under ordinary circumstances, with this attitude Michael would be poised for a fall as he came into an adult world. The extraordinary events of the trial and the discovery he makes throw him into a mental and moral wilderness in which he swings between complete emotional shutdown and overwhelming eruptions.

As a law student taking a seminar on the trials of those involved with the camps, he becomes exceedingly zealous about uncovering the ghastly actions and telling others about them. "Even when the facts took our breath away, we held them up triumphantly. Look at this!" Writing about them in the novel's present, Michael, who is the narrator, finds his behaviour at that time "repulsive." Zealousness gives way to numbness, as everyone in the courtroom seems to become detached from the witnesses' recounting of the horrors that had taken place. Michael says that this numbness extends to the rest of his life as well: "I stood outside myself and watched; I saw myself functioning at the university, with my parents and brother and sister and my friends, but inwardly I felt no involvement." On a skiing holiday he develops a high fever, and with it his emotional tumult returns: "All the questions and fears, accusations and self-accusations, all the horror and pain that had erupted during the trial and been immediately deadened were back, and back for good."

Long after the trial is over, Michael is still uncertain about his life, both past and future. He cannot decide what to do with his law degree; the trial showed him what a "grotesque oversimplification" are the roles of judge and prosecutor. Eighteen years later he is still asking himself about Hanna: "Did I not have my own accounting to demand of her? What about me?" His ambivalence about his connection to her life and death continues after she dies. "I was tormented," he thinks, "by the old questions of whether I had denied and betrayed her, whether I owed her something, whether I was guilty for having loved her. Sometimes I asked myself if I was responsible for her death. And sometimes I was in a rage at her and at what she had done to me." Michael is floundering in a Slough of Despond.

These are not the only questions Michael raises and does not answer. The overarching question is that of the moral responsibility of the second generation:

> What should our second generation have done, what should it do with the knowledge of the horrors of the extermination of the Jews? We should not believe we can comprehend the incomprehensible, we may not compare the incomparable, we may not inquire because to inquire is to make the horrors an object of discussion.... Should we only fall silent in revulsion, shame, and guilt? To what purpose?

What the second generation has done is to draw attention to those who have continued to attack Jews, and to old Nazis who have remained in office. "Pointing at the guilty parties," Michael says, "did not free us from shame, but at least it overcame the suffering we went through on account of it. It converted the passive suffering of shame into energy, activity, aggression." His own personal suffering over Hanna is quite another thing, however, and he does not get over that.

Part of the shame, and some of the accusation, is directed towards one's parents. While Michael himself has no reason to accuse his parents, many people have, and in the past they had "dissociated themselves from their parents and thus from the entire generation of perpetrators, voyeurs, and the willfully blind, accommodators and accepters...." He says he envied his fellow students who did this. (I must ask the question, why the envy? Was it perhaps easier to blame and hate someone than to have no one to blame?)

The inner conflict that some people must feel, between loving their parents and hating their behaviour during and after the war, is reflected in Michael's attitude towards Hanna, whom he loved and who was guilty of horrible crimes. He argues with himself that he did not know what she had done at the time of his affair. He says, "I tried to talk myself into the state of innocence in which children love their parents." He concludes that "the pain I went through because of my love for Hanna was, in a way, the fate of my generation, a German fate."

This seems to be a psychic situation without a cause and without a solution. Michael has no moral reason to feel guilty for loving Hanna, and yet he does feel shame. Linking this conflict to the ambivalent feelings others have for their parents for the same reason, one can see why it is a "German fate" of the second generation. Because it carries no moral responsibility and therefore no way of correcting it or cancelling it out, it seems like a vague, hovering angst that will never disappear. Michael says he writes the story of himself and Hanna "to be free of it, even if I never can be." The effect of this novel is to glimpse, if ever so slightly, this gnawing, endlessly miserable sense of the past that cannot be eradicated, just as the events that were the cause of it must remain alive to everyone's memories. Schlink offers no way out of this philosophical and emotional impasse, for there isn't one. This is a wilderness without egress.

As I puzzled about how to describe the various attempts to express the consequences of the Shoah for all of us, I faced another unalloyed horror: the September 11, 2001, terrorist attacks on New York and Washington. As Margaret Wente said in *The Globe and Mail* on September 12: "Someone took revenge on America, and America was helpless. Nothing there will ever be the same again."

Twice in half a century our world has been crucially affected by unprecedented outrages. In trying to understand this latest disaster, some questions that have been asked about the Holocaust, and the answers given, are relevant. Primo Levi asks, "Were we witnessing the rational development of an inhuman plan or a manifestation (unique in history and still unsatisfactorily explained) of collective madness? Logic intent on evil or the absence of logic? As so often happens in human affairs, the two alternatives coexisted."[17] In part, the answer depends on how you view ideology; many ideologies, I think, have their own logic within a world view that is dogmatic and mad.

What the Holocaust taught us, a lesson that should therefore mitigate our surprise at these terrorist attacks, is that the whole conceivable range of human behaviour has been stretched to the point where anything is possible. "Today," Steiner says, "it is difficult to conjecture a bestiality, a lunacy of oppression or sudden devastation, which would not be credible, which would not soon be located in the order of facts. Morally, psychologically, it is a terrible thing to be so un-astonished."[18] Jacques Ellul writes of a new morality, the "technological imperative," whereby "if it can be done, it must be done."[19] The systems by which the Jews were to be exterminated were not entirely perfected, but they might have been, given time; the use of a plane containing passengers as a bomb worked, although the human element—those heroes who we are told tried to prevent the plane from hitting its target and nevertheless died—crippled part of the plan. Technologies are being improved all the time. The question is, are we?

The world changed 50 years before the attack on the World Trade Center and on the Pentagon. Langer, referring to the conclusion of Elie Wiesel's *Night*, remarks that, "a world lies dead at our feet, a world we have come to know as our own as well as Wiesel's, and whatever civilization may be rebuilt from its ruins, the silhouette of its visage will never look the same."[20] As Wiesel says, "Nothing is innocent any more."[21]

Some of the innocence we have lost is the part that believed in a good society, a good culture, a good church. We know that the Allies did nothing to obstruct the Nazis by bombing the ovens or the rail lines, even though the fate of the Jews was known. We do not yet know, but are still trying to discover, why the churches, with a few fine exceptions, did nothing to help the Jews in word or deed. We know, from writers such as Rosemary Radford Ruether, that the seeds of anti-Semitism are found in the writings of some of the most central Christian writers, beginning with St. Paul. In fact, we must recognize that throughout the history of Christian civilization, the Jew has been anathematized, treated as wicked, blind, the other. In fact, when two bishops came to Hitler regarding his racial policy, he is reported to have responded that he "was only putting into effect what Christianity had preached and practised for 2000 years."[22] We must not remain indifferent to this legacy or we will perpetuate it.

In the past it has been our theology that perpetuates this attitude and still continues to do so in some religious circles. J.B. Metz, a contemporary German Catholic theologian, says that post-war theologians have taken little notice of the Holocaust and even now do not examine the roots of Christian theology in the light of it. I searched through my small library of books on contemporary theological issues, and could find only two writers who dealt with it at all. The rest ignored it completely.

As Langer says, there is a crack in the image of God that cannot be mended. We are beset by questions: Where was God when the Jews were suffering? What kind of God is this? Is it possible to hold a belief in God, and if so, what can we say? We are back to Ivan Karamazov's question to his brother Aloysha the monk: if, in order to bring about peace and happiness in the whole world order, it is necessary for one single child to suffer, would you undertake this? Aloysha's answer—that he would not do so, but that God who has shed his own blood for the world can forgive the perpetrators—will not do for the Jews, nor for Christians today who confront the Shoah.

Writers such as Wiesel, along with other thinkers both Jewish and Christian, pose either/or problems. Either God is powerful and cruel, or God is powerless and kind. Either God suffers with the suffering, or God is absent when needed. The God of old has been put on trial and found guilty. Either the Messiah has come, or he is not coming. The Messiah suffers and nothing changes, or he is all of us, and we are the only light of the world. Whatever attempts are made at answers, it is clear that the cracks in God's image, and in both the Christian and Jewish images of the world, are not mendable.

5

— CHOOSING THE SCAPEGOAT —

Hamm: What was she drivelling about?
Clov: She told me to go away, into the desert.
Hamm: Damn busybody!

Samuel Beckett, *Endgame*

People have got to have somebody to blame, Nichole.

Russell Banks, *The Sweet Hereafter*

The biblical creature who is the scapegoat has found its way into our common stock of images with rather unhappy results. While it hasn't changed its spots altogether, its original status and the significance of the ritual centred upon it have been lost over the centuries, leaving it in a weakened secular position. Today, when one thinks of the scapegoat, what comes most readily to mind is one word: victim.

I do not think that word ever came into God's mind when he instituted the annual ritual of atonement. What he said to Moses, as we read in the book of Leviticus, was that Aaron was to take the goat,

> lay his hands on its head and confess all the faults of the sons of Israel, all their transgressions and all their sins, and lay them to its charge. Having thus laid them on the goat's head, he shall send it out into the desert led by a man waiting ready, and the goat will bear all their faults away with it into a desert place.

Nothing survives in this barren desert.

What strikes me first about this rite is of course that the goat is blameless, and that the Israelites are contrite. The goat is only symbolically weighted down with sin, but this genuine act of confession and repentance is sufficient, and God forgives. Rabbi Irving Greenberg, writing about the Jewish holidays, emphasizes that it is the community that purges guilt, aided by the "unmerited grace" given by God. (This rite of the scapegoat is an ancient and almost forgotten one. Following the destruction of the Temple by the Romans in 70 CE, no sacrificial ceremonies were possible. Now in the synagogues the formal day of atonement has a different structure—although the retelling of the scapegoat ritual is part of it.) In a Christian theology held to be orthodox over many centuries, Christ was given the title " Saving Victim"—i.e., scapegoat.

Today a scapegoat could be anyone who takes the blame for someone else's evil acts. It may be someone who is driven by the powerful majority into the wilderness. The majority may be the guilty ones, but the scapegoat takes the punishment, thereby allowing the majority to believe that they are clean, upright. Since in our view of human nature no one is entirely innocent, the scapegoat will have faults too. They may not be the ones he or she is charged with, and they may not be so glaring as to deserve the hostility that the scapegoat receives. By contrast, the biblical scapegoat was blameless, and so not an object of scorn.

The most important difference between the sacrificial scapegoat of ancient times and today's is that those who cast someone out today have no sense of their own fault, and no contrition. The scapegoat is blamed, rather than symbolically burdened. Hence, for those doing the casting out there is no atonement, no grace, and no freedom. There is more hope for the scapegoat.

It is perhaps not pure chance (my selective reading) that the protagonist/scapegoats in the two novels discussed in this chapter are women. Apart from any negative attitude towards women that may be represented here as part of the social fabric of the novels (and of society itself), women are more likely objects of labelling and therefore verbal abuse. Their identity has been more fragile than men's: they often change their names on marriage, they are often identified as John's wife, Mary's mother, even old Sam's daughter. Because of status changes, they may be relabelled—Peter's widow. A woman with no close relatives would have had a difficult time of it in the past, as she would have had no identifying mark, unless she was a nurse or a teacher. If you are a nobody in your own right, you make an easy target, an obvious scapegoat.

The Sweet Hereafter, by Russell Banks, is a novel about many victims, many losers, and one scapegoat. On an early winter's day, the bus driven by Dolores Driscoll is taking the children to school in the village of Sam Dent. On the long hill leading into the village the bus suddenly swerves. It goes through the guard rail, tumbles down the hillside, and lands in an ice-covered sandpit filled with water. Fourteen of the children are killed. The novel begins after the accident, as four narrators describe what took place, what it means, and how they cope with it. As they speak, much more is revealed about the village and its inhabitants than their grieving and its consequences. Also, the condemnation and isolation of the scapegoat is only one of several forms of wilderness that appear as the book goes along.

The third narrator, Mitchell Stephens, is the one to give us a sense of the wilderness setting, because he is an outsider and trained to look. A New York negligence lawyer, he has come to Sam Dent even before the children's funerals have all taken place, to persuade the parents to sue whomever is responsible for the accident—the bus company, the town, the county perhaps. He admits that, even though he is an urban type and not keen on landscapes, the Adirondack region has a tremendous effect on him. He says it is "huge, endless, almost like being at sea"; after all, "we're talking six million acres of woods, mountains, and lakes, we're talking a region the size of the state of Vermont.... It's a landscape that controls you, sits you down and says, Shut up, pal. I'm in charge here."

In the middle of this landscape Stephens finds the habitations of the people Dolores says are "field-mouse poor": "patched-together houses with flapping plastic over the windows and sagging porches and wood-piles and rusting pickup trucks and junker cars parked in front, boarded-up roadside diners and dilapidated motels that got bypassed by the turn-pike...." Over the next few months his home in Sam Dent is one of these motels; there is no mention of any other visitor.

These two images of the wilderness—as vast and powerful, and as wasteland—come together in this story, as they so often do in rural areas in Canada and the United States. The scene of the accident itself is vast and bleak, as described by Billy Ansel, who was driving behind the bus when it went over: "The sky was ash gray and hung low over the mountains. Within a few hundred yards the spruce trees and pines in the wide valley below the road and the thick birch trees and the road itself quickly dimmed and then simply faded into sheets of falling snow and disappeared entirely from view." In this chill place Billy sees the bus halfway out of the sandpit, "like some huge dying yellow beast caught struggling to clamber out and frozen in the midst of the attempt," and the rescue workers "like lifetime prisoners in a Siberian gulag." Finally on the bank are the bodies of the children, covered in green blankets; "there was death, and it was everywhere on the planet and it was natural and forever; not just dying, perversely here and merely now." In a fierce land appears the worst kind of waste, that of the lives of the young.

The consequences of the accident are most devastating for the dead children's parents, whose lives are radically changed. As Billy says, "life has two meanings, one before the accident and one after." He reflects that "for us there was life, true life, real life, no matter how bad it had seemed, before the accident, and nothing that came after the accident resembled it in any important way."

Life was certainly bad for many of the bereaved people before the accident. There were the utterly poor families living in trailers and tarpaper shacks, beset by alcoholism and other unhappy habits, their lives just a step above miserable. Then there are Mitchell's clients, the Walkers and the Ottos, both of whom lost an only child, and his client *refusé*, Billy Ansel. The Walkers' motel is in dire straits, their marriage the same. Risa Walker and Billy have been meeting regularly a couple of times a week in a darkened motel room, and although they call it love, it is really only a comforting sexual relationship. Billy's wife, Lydia, "a fairy princess of a woman" according to Dolores, died of cancer four years back. Billy, a Vietnam vet, lost his only children, the twins Mason and Jessica, in the accident.

By contrast, the Ottos had been living a quiet, frugal life with their adopted son, Bear. They were civic-minded and concerned about the environment. Hartley made wood furniture and Wanda made ceramic pots. Wanda was finally pregnant. Before the accident in which Bear died their lives seemed to be contented.

All the other main characters in the novel come with their own burdens. Dolores Driscoll's husband, Abbott, had a stroke a few years back, leaving him with a serious speech impediment and confined to a wheelchair. While no one can make sense of what he says, Dolores says she understands him completely. Mitchell compares her to a puppeteer. The family's only income is from Dolores' driving of the school bus and other summer busing work.

Nichole, an eighth-grade student whose back was broken in the accident, is now also in a wheelchair. Before this she had been class president, captain of the school cheerleaders, and very well thought of as a babysitter. She has had a hidden life, however, of which she is wrenchingly ashamed. Whenever she and her father were alone together, he forced her into sexual touching—Nichole is not specific, says only that it is what girls do with their boyfriends. She is so horrified that she thinks often of killing herself. In public her father treats her in his normal fashion. The only person in her family that she really loves is her young sister Jenny; the others seem loveless and self-interested.

Mitchell has come to Sam Dent on a personal crusade. Unlike the ambulance-chasing lawyers propelled by greed, he wishes to make those faceless organizations, "some bungling corrupt state agency or some multinational corporation," whose lack of concern causes such accidents, pay for their indifference. It is they who are responsible for a world in which his daughter Zoe has become an addict, perhaps a hooker. To save her he must change the society that ruined her life. In physical terms, the wasteland in which Zoe lives and which he abhors is one of "filthy rat-infested apartments, garbage heaps with satanic altars lit by candles in a goat's skull on a TV in a corner." The internal wasteland Mitch inhabits is one of fury and helplessness at the fate of a daughter whose only connection with him is to call and wheedle him out of more money to fuel her desperately wasted life.

The seasons provide the metaphor that holds together all the action of this novel. In the winter it is the snow that at the beginning comes down like a "thin screen," allowing the accident to take place. Then the snow conceals the horrible traces of the disaster. Billy walks into the blinding snow, coming up the hill after helping the rescuers and seeing his own dead children. "I must have disappeared into it," he says, "just walked straight out of their reality into my own."

By springtime the snow has melted, and much more is revealed about the villagers than had been known at the time of the accident. Mitchell's attempts to persuade the parents and others to sue is the means of uncovering their real attitudes, strengths, and failings. The Walkers immediately agree to a suit because of their desperate need for money. As Mitchell asks them for the names of others who might be participants in the suit, Wendell comes forward with information about the misdeeds of many of the villagers. Of these grudges Mitchell says, "He'd probably kept them locked up inside himself for years, feeling guilty, and now for the first time in his life he believed he was entitled to lay about him." Nichole's parents, the Burnells, are greedy, eager to collect the money for themselves, although it is Nichole who has suffered. The Ottos will take part in the suit because they are angry, and justifiably so; there seems to be no ulterior motive.

Then there are those who are unwilling to sue. Billy says that nothing can help him in his grief. He tries to persuade the Burnells to drop their suit because he thinks the whole town has gone crazy dreaming up whom they can sue next. When Mitchell approaches Dolores and Abbott, saying that if she joins the suit he can clear her name, Abbott's response is that the people who have always known Dolores must be her judges, not strangers. If she has committed a crime it is against the village. So they refuse to sue. Even young Nichole does not think it is right to sue the state. She could understand why the parents who had lost children might want to sue, even though this "somehow didn't seem right, either." But for her parents to sue, when she is alive—"I didn't understand that at all," she reflects, "and I really knew it wasn't right. Not if I was, like they said, truly lucky." Still, her parents agree, and Nichole's deposition is considered to be crucial to the case. She feels "greedy and dishonest" about it.

It is her deposition that turns the tide. Mitchell has prepared her, and she is supposed to describe what her life was like before the accident, and what it has become. She has said that she remembers nothing of the accident itself, so she is not a material witness. Taking everyone by surprise, she declares during the deposition that she is beginning to remember what happened. She says that she recalls seeing the speedometer registering 72 miles per hour when Dolores was going down the hill. This kills the suit, first because no one wants to sue Dolores, and second, because Dolores has no money to give anyone. The state, the county, and everyone else are off the hook.

Nichole has taken herself off the hook, too—and put her father on it. The deposition is her revenge, and from now on she holds the power over him. He can never take his own revenge, because she is the be-loved invalid and the keeper of his terrible secret.

At the same time, in a sort of parallel to the deposition, Mitchell Stevens finds himself off the hook in his relationship to Zoe. She has called him for money, this time claiming that she has AIDS. Mitchell knows that he will finally be able to tell whether Zoe is lying or not, and this will free him "from love." It was his love that kept him from know-ing whether to believe her or not, and from acting in the light of what was true. Now he can act. He says this, however: "She'd played her final card with me; she could no longer keep me from being who I am. Mitchell Stephens, Esquire." Neither Nichole nor Mitchell, in taking control, has gained anything in contentment, though their separate agonies have been removed.

Owing to the dropped suit, the Walkers have had to sell their mo-tel. They are getting a divorce. Nothing has changed for the Ottos, except that they have a new baby. Billy Ansel is relieved that the village is no longer driven by greed. The suit has not affected him personally: it is the loss of his children that has turned him to drinking. As Dolores says, "He had been a noble man; and now he was ruined." The village has lots of empty houses and trailers, some people are dealing drugs, and one parent has been in a mental institution. "A town needs its chil-dren for a lot more than it thinks," Dolores says.

Dolores' life has changed already, but at the end of the book we are left to wonder how it will change even more drastically. Right from the time of the accident, she has not been driving the school bus, and she was not asked to drive the mail in the summer. She no longer shops in Sam Dent, and she tries to keep out of everyone's way. At the end of the summer, however, she decides to take Abbott to the county fair for his annual treat, the demolition derby. It is here that she meets Billy, drunk, who tells her what the whole village has known for some time: that Nichole has stated she was speeding when the accident occurred. She finally realizes that they blame her, just as she knows Nichole is wrong. The effect of this revelation is to make her feel both solitary and strong, entirely separate from the people of Sam Dent, and having become, along with the other participants in the accident alive and dead, part of "a town of solitaries living in a sweet hereafter."

Dolores is singled out from those other sufferers, however, in two narrative moments at the demolition derby. There is, first, the contrast between her arrival with Abbott in a wheelchair and Nichole's with her parents. People turn their heads away when they see Dolores, and no one offers to help her lift Abbott's wheelchair up the stairs to the top of the stands until Billy comes along. As Sam Burnell says to his daughter, "People have got to have somebody to blame." When Nichole arrives people begin to touch her and to clap, "and she waved one hand back and forth slowly, like a saint in a religious procession or something," says Dolores. Several men lifted her wheelchair up the stairs "like it was a throne."

The next episode—by this time Dolores has learned why people are not speaking to her—concerns her old station wagon, nicknamed Boomer by the children she used to carry in it at the start of her busing career. Boomer has been bought by a friend and entered in the derby. The whole town cheers every time Boomer is hit, and all the cars are determined to destroy it. Then the game changes, and Boomer becomes the hero, destroying the last two cars to win. Dolores does not cheer. The symbolism of the villagers' mixed feelings about Dolores is obvious. Less obvious is the parallel with the "saintly" Nichole, who is intent on destroying her father's life as revenge for his vile behaviour.

This book is about waste—needless, cruel, mindless, hopeless—revealed by the tragedy and its aftermath. It is the wilderness of the prophets in its desolation and pitilessness—and of the vast emptiness of the no man's land into which the scapegoat is driven. The death of the children causes the quiet desperation of people's lives to appear in public. Although it may seem to Dolores that the town must have its children in order to survive, it was in fact "living and partly living" well before the children died. Russell Banks points no finger, offers no remedies, makes no moral statements. Everything that needs to be said about how people live in a wilderness that is both solitary and wasted is there in the lives of these people as they react to the worst thing that could ever happen to them. In this scenario the scapegoat doesn't take the sin away.

In *The Sweet Hereafter*, the scapegoat is the victim, the accused, the one who bears all the blame because there has to be an explanation of how this disaster occurred. The symbolic nature of the scapegoat is almost lost in favour of the rational. The next novel I will introduce has a closer, although perverse, connection to the biblical idea of a scapegoat that traditionally carries off the collective sins of a society.

As I've grown older I've watched the dying out of traditions with sad dismay. It isn't just the major rites and ceremonies such as the religious ones—even the loss of the minor social things bothers me. When I was a youngster we ate fish on Friday, roast beef on Saturday, chicken on Sunday. On Saturday we went to the market and washed the car, while on Friday the baking was done—all this in preparation for Sunday, when the day was free after church to read, go for a walk, and listen to the radio without fail. Nothing precluded the march past of Jack Benny and his gang, followed by Fred Allen with Senator Claghorn and company, and last, Edgar Bergen and Charlie McCarthy, usually with that other lovable wooden-headed chap, Mortimer Snerd. Today few people who missed out on that period of our history would believe that this routine way of life was lively and fun.

Rummaging through the family papers I discovered many of the diaries of my great-grandfather Walker (b. 1836) from the years 1881 to 1928. They aren't very exciting, but they show the routines of a life that seems to have been contented. Every day he began by noting the weather and the temperature. In his later years after he retired I read that he and his wife took a drive every pleasant afternoon from 5:00 to 6:00, either in the buggy or in the car, driven by one of the great-nephews. On the anniversary of any of their children's deaths, they put flowers on the grave. I also discovered my grandmother's visiting book, listing the day of every week in which each St. Catharines matron was "at home." My grandmother's day was Wednesday.

There were other habits, probably rigidly enforced by the social bluebloods of Ontario towns as elsewhere. If you were excluded from this fashionable circle, it was because you didn't know the difference between right—white gloves on Sunday—and wrong—no gloves at all. Right was saying, "How do you do?" Wrong was a casual "Hello." None of these failings would get you run out of town, or even ostracized. Still, it would be better if you learned the correct way to do things.

There were, I remember, traditional ways of thinking, too, that were more like superstitions, such as not stepping on a crack or walking under a ladder. Don't let a black cat cross your path; it's bad luck unless you have one. (We almost always did.) During a thunderstorm we covered all the mirrors and sat in an inner room if the storm was severe. Everyone knew you shouldn't try anything risky on Friday the 13th. Many people still agree.

Despite these quaint customs and beliefs, we in the West have never lived in an entirely tradition-bound world. Education wrests young people's minds away from the unquestioned beliefs and behaviour of their ancestors, although it may take a couple of generations for the old ways to go. It is hard to imagine how it might be to live in a society that depends primarily on habits and beliefs with no apparently rational foundation, although those societies exist today. It isn't too difficult to imagine, however, the existence of a scapegoat there, one who is singled out for disobedience to the society's norms.

Lives of the Saints, a novel by Nino Ricci, tells the story of a young woman, Cristina, who has been left with her son Vittorio in their native village of Valle del Sole in the Apennines, while her husband Mario works in America to earn money for the family. The story is told in retrospect by Vittorio, who was seven years old when the central events took place. So a now-wiser narrator is able to set the story in an ironic framework, as the young Vittorio tries and fails to interpret what is going on around him. Reader and Vittorio both learn gradually what has happened, with the reader putting it all together much earlier than Vittorio does. This practice introduces pathos, and although Cristina is the main scapegoat, eventually Vittorio takes her place, left out in the wilderness by himself.

What we gradually discover is that Cristina has been having an affair with a German soldier who stayed at her father's house briefly during the war. Since then they have met in a neighbouring village, but one day he writes that he is coming to visit her in Valle del Sole that very day. Unable to stop him, Cristina meets him in the stable, where they have intercourse. Unfortunately she is bitten by a snake there, and must go to hospital. The snake and the blue-eyed stranger are observed by Vittorio, who doesn't understand anything except that his mother has been struck by the evil eye—the villagers tell him that is what the snake conveys.

Valle del Sole is a village held back by poverty and lack of influence from the usual services and comforts of late-twentieth-century life. There is no electricity, no plumbing, no telephone. Only the restaurant owner has a car, and the inter-village bus is a converted truck. Communication between villages seems to be so slight that one dislikes and envies the other, even though *invidia* (envy), we are told by the narrator, is the sin to be avoided. Do not let on how well your harvest has done, or brag about how many children you have. If you do so, the evil eye may fall on you and destroy the one, kill the other. The evil eye is more powerful than any deity:

> It was drawn towards you merely by a certain lack of vigilance, a small flouting of fate, a crack in the door it might slither through, fangs bared, to catch you by surprise; and its fickleness made it deadly and all-powerful, like fate itself, a force which knew no masters, neither God nor the devil.

This enclosed world of routine everyday labour is enlivened by religious festivals and holidays, and dramatized by superstitions. Even the poorest find some money to help pay for the village saint's feast day: it is expected. Religion mixes indiscriminately with folkways; the reason to choose one over the other is whichever has the most powerful magic. When it appears that Cristina is pregnant, her friend Giuseppina tells her to deal with her pregnancy either by confessing to the priest or, since she won't do that, performing a blood ritual with a dead chicken. To avoid the evil eye, one wears garlic or wolves' teeth and places goats' horns over the doorway. For some serious problems one can resort to *la strega*, the witch who lives in the ruins above the village and makes helpful potions.

Cristina's affair has been known for some time, but, as Vittorio says, the real story begins with the snake. (There's the ur-example of myth-over-reason: a reminder of the first-woman, first-snake story and what that meant for all of us miserable descendants.) Its bite casts a different light on her activity: Cristina is cursed, and the effect is contagious. Giuseppina says, "You'll bring a curse on everyone around you." Gradually the village begins to avoid her. On San Camilla's day no one comes to visit her and her father, the mayor. Only her two oldest friends turn up later, but they keep their distance near the door. People turn their eyes away as they pass her sitting outside her house. Gradually the house itself becomes silent, as Cristina and her father have very little to say to each other. Vittorio says that the only sound is his mother crying at night in her bedroom. Grandfather leaves the house and sits alone on the restaurant's terrace every day. Vittorio overhears people speaking about his mother, but he does not understand their meaning.

On Christmas day Grandfather insists she go to church. Afterwards several old friends come to visit bringing pastries, as is the custom. Vittorio says:

> Some consensus had been reached, it seemed, at dozens of houses across the village, my mother's presence at church, debated and discussed over Christmas dinner, finally taken perhaps as some kind of a sign, the sign of the repentance and guilt which the villagers had no doubt long been waiting for....

Grandfather, however, says they came to laugh. He is ashamed to walk through town, and he explodes with anger, saying, among other maledictions, that he wishes she had never been born. In his rage he falls and breaks his leg and his hip and is confined to bed. In his misery, it is he who drives Cristina out, telling her that he won't let her house her bastard child with him. It seems that she had already planned to go to America, but not until after the child was born. Now, once the passports are ready, she prepares to leave abruptly. The reader must assume that she is in a hurry because she will deliver the child fairly soon.

The last straw for Grandfather is when he realizes that she is not going to join her husband in America, but her lover. He curses her out of the house, and she and Vittorio get on the bus that will bring them to the port and their ship. Cristina's parting words are a riposte at all those who have condemned her. "'Fools!' she shouted now. 'You tried to kill me but you see I'm still alive. And now you came to watch me hang, but I won't be hanged, not by your stupid rules and superstitions. You are the ones who are dead, not me." She concludes with a curse: "I pray to God that he wipes this town and all its stupidities off the face of the earth!'"

Valle del Sole is an unprogressive place, bound by tradition and terrified by omens and superstitions that have long trails: even Cristina's husband, Mario, in America refuses to take her child, wants it put in an orphanage. Yet it is not only their hidebound attitudes that condemn Cristina; her own character is as much to blame. She is an outsider already, believing that the villagers are idiots and jackasses, and not restraining herself from showing what she thinks. In their words she is "holding her nose up like a queen"—she speaks proud words, and has no shame. Near the end of the story when she says, "The only mistake I made was that I didn't leave this hell a dozen years ago, when I had the chance," we realize that the village has watched this affair going on in their midst for a very long time. Cristina is unbending in her belief that she can do as she likes, and she makes no concessions to the popular sense of decency.

Cristina's death would probably have left the villagers saying that it was fated, right from the moment that the snake bit her. (I am speculating; this is not in the novel.) A terrible storm on board ship causes her a severely upset stomach and vomiting, which in turn brings on the birth of the baby. The baby lives; Cristina dies from loss of blood, combined with the lack of full attention from the drunken doctor and the nurse who is sick herself. She is buried at sea.

Vittorio is left alone. Except for one friend in the village, Fabrizio, he has been alone throughout his life, however. Since the snake affair it has been worse. Fabrizio has been told not to associate with him, and the son of Cristina's best friend fought him. A group of boys trapped him under the pretext of initiating him into their gang, but Fabrizio rescued him before they could hurt him. His only comforter was his teacher, who read to him from a book about the lives of the saints. The book is her parting gift to him. His grandfather's final words to him are, "I hope to God she doesn't ruin your life the way she's ruined hers."

After his mother dies, Vittorio develops a high fever and pneumonia and spends a long time in an American hospital. His father "cried without shame" when he first saw him, and comes to visit him daily. Once he is better, he leaves with his father holding his baby sister, and travels on a "coal-dust-filled train...across a desolate landscape, bleak and snow-covered for as far as the eye could see." They are headed for the famous Sun Parlour of Canada that the people of Valle del Sole talk about, where his father lives. One is left at the end of the novel in some doubt as to how things will turn out for Vittorio (this is the first of a trilogy): is he to be another scapegoat like his mother, or will life improve in his new home? To the native of Valle del Sole the last incident of the novel would be an omen. As Vittorio fingers his lucky coin given him by Luciano, whose life it had saved in the war, it slips through the ship's rails and falls into the ocean.

Cristina's fate is similar to that of Hagar, the slave-girl mother of Abraham's first son, Ishmael. Hagar, once she is pregnant, becomes proud and treats her mistress, Sarah with disdain, a characteristic Cristina shares. Hagar escapes twice to the wilderness, in both cases driven out by Sarah's jealousy—the same *invidia* that the villagers are capable of, and which likely forms part of their hatred of Cristina. Cristina's father turns against her, as Abraham does against Hagar. Hagar lives with Ishmael in the wilderness and eventually finds him an Egyptian wife and together they found a dynasty. Vittorio is headed for a new life in a different land. No dynastic hopes are promised yet; the sequels will provide the answer to that question.

The tensions in both situations are irresolvable. Now that Sarah has her own son, Ishmael must go; both sons cannot inherit. The only recourse is the uncertain no man's land of the wilderness, in which divine and not human support is what must be counted on. In Cristina's case, there are two children, the legitimate and the bastard to come. Neither can in a sense inherit, because her libertine behaviour causes her to be excluded from village life, and eventually thrown out altogether. The villagers' hatred of her is justified by traditional beliefs in omens and spells. These beliefs, compounded with her devil-may-care attitude, make her a scapegoat and send her out into her final wilderness.

The symbol of the scapegoat as a ritual offering has lost its noblest central meanings and become a sign, a receptacle for anger and hatred. Signs such as this are arbitrary: they can turn up anywhere. If you try to look for a foundation for beliefs in signs and omens, such as these villagers have, you cannot find it. Many thousands of years ago, there may have been a religious world view that included such things, but it has vanished—if it ever existed. Today the biblical scapegoat has also become, as both of these novels show, a sign of someone who has been targeted, singled out, excluded, for reasons that are untenable, violent, bigoted, or thoughtless. The result for the scapegoat is clear, but for society it is less so. One thing seems evident: for those doing the scapegoating there is no change and no reprieve. The biblical ritual implied a fresh start with sins forgiven, a chance to correct one's life, and for the whole community to improve. In Banks' and Ricci's novels there is no admission of sin or wrongdoing on the part of the community, and the direction of movement, if any, is downhill. In Leviticus there is a clear distinction between the scapegoat in the wilderness and the community. These modern novels blur the edges in that, having driven out the scapegoat, the community remains in the wilderness, unforgiven and unlovely. More and more, the bleak and nasty aspects of the wilderness seem to be taking over the world.

6

— THE PROFANE WILDERNESS —

She is down and will rise no more,
the virgin of Israel.
There she lies all alone on her own soil,
with no one to lift her up.

Amos 5:2

What is that sound high in the air
Murmur of maternal lamentation
Who are those hooded hordes swarming
Over endless plains, stumbling in cracked earth
Ringed by the flat horizon only
What is the city over the mountains
Cracks and reforms and bursts in the violet air
Falling towers
Jerusalem Athens Alexandria
Vienna London
Unreal

T.S. Eliot, "What the Thunder Said," *The Waste Land*

...so shall the world goe on,
To good malignant, to bad men benigne,
Under her own waight groaning...

Milton, *Paradise Lost*, xii. 337-339

...this howling desart...

Edward Johnson, *Wonder-Working Providence*
of Sions Saviour in New England (1654)

Ever since T.S. Eliot published *The Waste Land* in 1922, the term has been adopted by innumerable people, from radical students to disenchanted middle-aged bourgeois, from preachers to secular thinkers. Most of them have probably never read the poem, but its implicit meaning resonates with them nonetheless. Those who lived through two world wars and, in the case of Americans, another contentious engagement in Vietnam, have added their understandings to Eliot's. Existentialists living in Europe after the Second World War believed they lived in the wasteland, while most of the rest of the world patched itself together and tried to formulate a recipe for peace in our time and everyone else's.

Those who did read the poem knew that Eliot wasn't minting a new phrase; in fact, the building blocks for his dry, cryptically resonant verse were the tales and sighs and laments of many earlier writers and storytellers. Although Eliot's wasteland was different, it came from history and led us back into history and myth.

The story that unified the poem was taken from an episode in the Arthuriad. A very early version of the quest of Percival to find the Holy Grail has him staying overnight in the castle of the Maimed King, a person whose illness is contiguous (or homologous perhaps) with the predicament of his lands that are now devoid of life. If Percival will only ask the Maimed King what ails him, that is, inquire kindly about his well-being, then the king and his lands will both be restored to health. Sadly, Percival's mamma has brought him up not to be nosey, so he doesn't ask. The reader knows in advance that Percival is not the man for the Grail.

The connection between the afflictions of a country and its king is one way of showing how the wasteland can be associated with a desolation of the individual. Long before the prose *Percival* came into existence, the Hebrew prophets knew plenty about this condition. They drew their own conclusions: the barren land came about as a result of the degradation of people's wills and behaviour.

Then, with a quick shift, a striking new metaphor was created. It wasn't the land that was at fault, although it was doomed to be blighted and laid bare; it was the city. The city stood for its people, those whom the prophets accused of an assortment of evils. The wanderers in the wilderness had settled down and made of their cities a wasteland. In

some situations, it was the enemies' cities that were to become wastelands because of the evils they had inflicted on God's people. The metaphor grew as it must, because it wasn't the cities' fault entirely, but that
of people everywhere; the wasteland was the whole country, it was Israel, it was Judah.

One of the most moving of all poems is Isaiah's song of the vineyard, in which God bemoans the wicked results of his good planting:

Let me sing to my friend
the song of his love for his vineyard.
My friend had a vineyard
on a fertile hillside.
He dug the soil, cleared it of stones,
and planted choice vines in it.
In the middle he built a tower,
he dug a press there too.
He expected it to yield grapes,
but sour grapes were all that it gave.

And now, inhabitants of Jerusalem
And men of Judah,
I ask you to judge
between my vineyard and me.
What could I have done for my vineyard
that I have not done?
I expected it to yield grapes.
Why did it yield sour grapes instead?

Very well, I will tell you
what I am going to do to my vineyard:
I will take away its hedge for it to be grazed on,
and knock down its wall for it to be trampled on.
I will lay it waste, unpruned, undug;
overgrown by the briar and the thorn.
I will command the clouds
to rain no rain on it.
Yes, the vineyard of the Lord Sabaoth
is the House of Israel,

and the men of Judah
that chosen plant.
He expected justice, but found bloodshed,
integrity, but only a cry of distress.

Ezekiel, too, speaks of Israel as the vine that has been put in the wilderness and has dried up. Jeremiah, writing in Judah before the arrival of the Babylonian conquerors, condemns Jerusalem and Judah as wastelands. On another occasion a drought dries up the land; God tells Jeremiah that the drought has come on account of Judah's sins: "They take such pleasure in wandering, they cannot control their feet!"

The city/nation as wilderness is linked to another image, that of adultery. Jeremiah condemns Judah and Israel as harlots, and Jerusalem with them. Isaiah also calls Jerusalem a harlot; the daughters of Zion are harlots. Even adultery is a metaphor, though, for a daunting list of additional sins: idolatry, arrogance, rebelliousness, obstinacy, cruelty, injustice, greediness and luxurious living, bribery. The overarching sin from which all of these emanate is faithlessness, turning away from God, either to other gods or to selfish desires. Punishment will be the result.

In all these descriptions the picture of the wilderness as rolling pasture, fertile most of the time and visited by rain seasonally, is absent. Instead the prophets describe a parched land, uninhabited and uninhabitable, with wasted crops and roaming wild beasts. Barren as it is, worse is to come: a scorching wind will blow over the land and the whole world will be made waste and void. The most devastating picture of the land's destruction is the one about Edom, in which even the water turns to pitch, thorns grow up in the ruins of cities, and unpleasant creatures—vipers and kites—make it their home. Again, Isaiah presents a vivid picture of the action God will take against the whole earth for its wickedness:

See how [the LORD] lays the earth waste,
makes it a desert, buckles its surface,
scatters its inhabitants,
priest and people alike, master and slave,
mistress and maid, seller and buyer,
lender and borrower, creditor and debtor.
Ravaged, ravaged the earth,

despoiled, despoiled,
as [the LORD] has said.
The earth is mourning, withering,
the world is pining, withering,
the heavens are pining away with the earth.
The earth is defiled
under its inhabitants' feet,
for they have transgressed the law, violated the precept,
broken the everlasting covenant.

This imagery makes Eliot's seem like a picnic. There is no shadow at all under these red rocks.

It seems as though the prophets have taken the image of wilderness of the Exodus, and, playing upon its dark side, used it for alarming effect. The wasteland envisioned in Isaiah 34 is almost a match in its violence and bleakness for that predicted in Leviticus 26, although not all the details of destruction are the same. The metaphor of Israel as a harlot parallels the debauchery episode in Numbers 25. Ezekiel's image of a wandering flock with its bad shepherds is an inversion of the memory of the faithful flock guided by its divine shepherd. Jeremiah's instruction from God to give the people a bitter cup to drink "to make them into a desolation and a waste" contrasts with the occasion when the bitter water of Marah is purified in the wilderness. The idolatry of Israel that Amos condemns is directly related to the idolatry of the Exodus.

As a result of their faithlessness, God is going to withdraw from his people, leave them to their own devices and perils. Conquerors will come, and God will not help. He is fed up with them, and this time he will not come when they claim to repent: "Even if Moses and Samuel were standing in my presence I could not warm to this people!" This is a world made profane.

I should make clear at the outset that when I say the wilderness has become profane, it is not at all the same as saying it is secularized. In a secular realm, which is the Western world as most people know it today, there is no sense of, or loss of, the sacred. Whatever was formerly of divine import has disappeared from consciousness or concern.

Not so with the world seen as profane. To be profane, it has to be a profanation of something. There is at least a memory of former sacredness—and probably very strong feelings against it, since what

was once sacred is now the complete opposite. Dr. T.R.V. Murti, a re-
nowned professor of Hindu philosophy, used to say to his students over
and over, as the basis for the argument about the oneness of ultimate
reality, "Two things must stand on a common platform in order to
be compared." The sacred and the profane stand together. (As to the
nature of the platform, that is for someone like Paul Tillich—or Professor Murti—to elucidate.)

A totally secular world is a poor, thin place compared even to a
profane one. There is no platform on which it can stand, no destiny to
which it can point. On the contrary, in a place where the sacred has
been profaned, the tunnel towards a new vision of sacredness is open-
ended, even if it is cluttered with refuse and graffiti and loose bricks.
One may have to do a lot of digging, and perhaps a lifetime may not be
enough. No one knows what is at the end of the tunnel, except that it is
probably not an atmosphere like the one you left behind.

One person's sacred world or image or credo may be for another
utterly profane, something she has rejected, although she is still connected to it by lingering anger and accusations. The person who continues to attach sacred meaning to this world may be infuriated at those
who profane it. God is like this in Isaiah, his feelings towards his wayward chosen a mixture of anger and self-pity. (What did I do wrong? I
tried my best.) A lot of anger often comes from those profaners who
may still regret the loss of the sacred vision they once entertained.

The wilderness as wasteland is not an image for secular thinkers—
Where is the sacred? Where is the common ground? To the secular mind,
refuse is refuse, not the cast-off clothing of old idols. Graffiti are the
public statements of the young on the only platforms they can claim. I
used to think that the ever-present appearance of the f-word in public
toilets and elsewhere was profanity; after watching episodes of the TV
series *The Sopranos* I realize it is part of the same group slang that my
teenage gang used to come up with, when we used words like "damn"
and "stupid" and other breezier terms I have forgotten. What is truly
profane is that when you use the word "profane," the only thing people
can think of is dirty words.

We have already caught a whiff of the way in which the wilderness
has been profaned and become a wasteland. It is visible in *King*, in both
a physical and inhumane way. This is the wasteland of greed and disre-

gard, as we see it again in the bounty hunters of *Cold Mountain*. All the sins of the city appear in *The Sweet Hereafter*, with the underlying despair that conditions them. *The Reader* reveals the profanity of sticking to one's duty rather than saving lives, and in *The Gates of the Forest*, the villagers' anger against Gregor exemplifies in miniature the ultimate profanity against human beings that was the Holocaust. So, we are already prepared for this image to appear in all its ugly distortion of the world that God said was good.

Plenty of excellent writers understand and unfold the contemporary secular world for us; yet they do not know this profane wilderness. Two of the finest writers to appear in the last half of the last century know it very well, however, and give us pictures of our present wasteland that rival the biblical. Philip Roth and Samuel Beckett, both novelists and the latter a playwright as well, compel me, each in his own way, to enter so fully into their fictional worlds that I can never emerge the same person as I went in. Beckett's deadpan audacity and bizarre telling allow me to have some distance from the worlds he presents, until my mind starts to go beyond his imagery and his characters to their unique platform, and then I am hornswoggled. Roth's world seduces by its very similarity to everything I know, disarming through the rapidity and perspicacity with which he gives us his people, the gentle irony in the snap-crackle of his descriptions. This is a world from which I may never escape.

In Roth's *American Pastoral*, the narrator, Skip Zuckerman, is a writer who slips in and out of the story so noiselessly that you almost forget him. The story he is going to tell us is kick-started by a meeting he has with a childhood sports hero, Seymour Levov, "the Swede," many years later. To his dismay he finds that the great Swede has deteriorated into a cheerful, mindless conservative with a painlessly boring life, a "big jeroboam of self-contentment." As Skip saw it at first, with his three sports-keen sons and a second wife, the Swede's life seemed to be "just unraveling for the Swede like a fluffy ball of yarn." That is, until sometime, not much later, Skip meets his old ping-pong rival, Jerry, the Swede's younger brother, just come from the Swede's funeral. Jerry tells Skip the real story. The contented life the Swede had made for himself, in charge of the family business, with a beautiful wife, Dawn, and a clever, loving daughter Meredith ("Merry"), was shattered in 1968 when Merry set off a bomb in the general store/post office of their village, killing a doctor who was collecting his mail. Merry has been in hiding ever since. The Swede was killed, says Jerry, by the anguish he felt but never allowed to surface.

Skip is appalled at how wrong he was about the Swede: "I whose vanity is that he is never naive, was more naive by far than the guy I was talking to…the story that is tragic and awful and impossible to ignore, the ultimate reunion story, and I missed it entirely." He decides to write a "realistic chronicle" of the Swede's life, how it might have been. Exit the narrator, for the most part.

Roth (not the narrator) has framed his novel in three sections, called "Paradise Remembered," "The Fall," and "Paradise Lost." Because of ironic placement and differing points of view, this is not an updated account of either the Genesis story or Milton's, although they are the launch pads. Taken together, there are four, perhaps five, different views of the profane world (and not all of them appear after the fall), set against opposing views of what was, or is, sacred. One person's wasteland is another's dream. Looming over all of these stands the great sacred vision that is the American pastoral.

The Swede's family is a cast of dreamers, each living in a sacred past or a present ideology. Only Jerry is a realist, perhaps, but hardly a model for living, with his four wives, his bulldog attitude to everyone, and his shutting off of the past. His eulogy of his brother is, however, the only interpretation of the Swede's life that Skip has to go on, so that is the novel's take on our hero.

The story is fully and centrally the Swede's, and it moves along as the mind often does, through a present that is interrupted demandingly by thoughts of the past. After the bomb—the fall—the Swede's entire present is taken up with thoughts of Merry. He remembers her as a funny, loving, skinny child who developed an embarrassing stutter and tried everything possible to overcome it. He remembers how the stutter disappeared when she became angry and politically engaged, as she shouted insults at the TV image of Lyndon Johnson. How she argued with her liberal, anti-war father about what should be done about Vietnam, and how finally at 16, to protest the war, she set her bomb. The doctor's death was unintended.

Five years after the bomb, the Swede has news of Merry and goes to find her. He knows he cannot tell Dawn about this, as he thinks back on her recent treatment for suicidal depression and her new-found appetite for life. The news would shatter her fragile state. He is shocked by the bleak and decrepit state in which he finds Merry living in a squat. He comes home to give a dinner party, but all he can think of is Merry, until he makes some fresh unwelcome discoveries in the present.

To grasp what has happened to the Swede we must see how he got there. He believes, like Lear, that he is a man more sinned against than sinning. His faults are common ones, and in themselves noble: he wishes to make a good life for himself and his family, and he goes to any self-effacing lengths to make sure that they are happy. As a start, he comes under his father's thumb, who takes him into the glove-making business, starting him at the bottom and teaching him everything about how to make a perfect glove. The business is successful, and the Swede grows rich.

Then the first wasteland appears, and it is his father, Lou Levov, who sees it and cries doom in language that sounds like the biblical prophets:

> In Newark corruption is the name of the game. What is new, number one, is race; number two, taxes. Add *that* to the corruption, *there's* your problem.... Race is just the icing on the cake. Streets aren't cleaned. Burned-out cars nobody takes away. People in abandoned buildings. *Fires* in abandoned buildings. Unemployment. Filth. Poverty. More filth. More poverty. Schooling nonexistent. Schools a disaster. On every street corner dropouts. Dropouts doing nothing. Dropouts dealing drugs. Dropouts looking for trouble. The projects—don't get me started on the projects. Police on the take. Every kind of disease known to man.

Sounding like the voice of God, Lou says, "As far back as the summer of '64 I told my son, 'Seymour, get out.' 'Get out,' I said, but he won't listen. Paterson goes up, Elizabeth goes up, Jersey City goes up. You got to be blind in both eyes not to see what is next. And I told this to Seymour."

Now Lou and Sylvia live in Miami, take cruises and visit Seymour and Dawn once a year. Lou's sacred realm, today a wasteland, was the glove factory where he set his desk in the centre of the sewing room so he could catch problems as soon as they happened. His sacred time was when rich women owned 24 pairs of gloves, and he sold Newark Maid gloves to the army and to the glossiest stores in New York. In those days, workers were good and genial, gloves were made to perfection. Then came the riots, and all was profaned by "taxes, corruption and race."

Lou is an ideologue, a one-dimensional thinker for whom things are either black or white, these days mostly black. He began his working life at 14 in a tannery dyeing and sorting hides, graduated to selling from a push-cart, and eventually bought an old factory and made fine gloves. As the narrator says, "What was amazing was how civil he could sometimes still manage to be."

Chronologically, Merry is the next one to single out a wasteland, and it is the one she lives in before the bomb. To see what Merry denounces as her father's wasteland we have to look at it first through the Swede's eyes, because to him it is the sacred life, the American pastoral enacted in Old Rimrock, New Jersey, where he lives. His enchanted life began early; he was a handsome, golden-haired Jewish hero in his high school, a three-letter sports star, with the equanimity and modesty that made people look up to him. For the rest of his life, he seems to be obliged to keep up that godlike image, no matter what happened to him. Until the bomb, everything that happened befitted the image: he marries Dawn Dwyer, a former Miss New Jersey, and moves into an old stone house on a hundred acres among the pedigreed settlers—the amazing achievement of a Jewish boy and a Catholic girl with lowly beginnings who are accepted (or at least not rejected) by establishment Protestant America. Dawn proves that she is not just a pretty face by raising prize-winning Simmenthal cattle. One of the Swede's happiest memories is of Dawn and Merry bringing in the cattle; on one near-disastrous occasion they are able to rescue Count, the prize bull, from an island in a swamp on which he had been stranded, inching him forward for hours through the mud. Not only does the happy family live an idyllic life in the house Swede had always wanted to have, but also he has kept the business alive and thriving through the Newark riots when other buildings were being set on fire and destroyed. He truly believes that his life was as good as it gets.

When the Vietnam war became the central controversy in American life, the Swede declares himself against it, even goes to Washington with a group of businessmen to make their views known. At the same time,

Merry enters her miserable teenage years stuttering, overweight, and politically alert, antagonistic to the war and the way of life of Americans whom she thinks support it. It is her own family's bourgeois life she rails against, their indifference to what is happening in Vietnam, where "America is b-blowing little b-babies to b-b-b-b-bits... You don't care enough to let it upset a single day of yours." Later, as she spends more time with Communist friends, she rails against her father:

> You think everything that is f-foreign to you is b-bad. Did you ever think that there are some things that are f-foreign to you that are good?... I think extreme is to continue on with life as usual when this kind of craziness is going on, when people are b-being exploited left, right, and center, and you can just go on and get into your suit and tie every day and go to work. As if nothing is happening. That is extreme. That is extreme s-s-s-stupidity, that is what that is.

When the Swede finds Merry five years after the bombing, in a derelict building among abandoned warehouses below the highway that runs through Newark, she has changed completely, from an abrasive activist to an isolated, gently introspective pacifist. She has left her Communist friends and beliefs and has become a Jain. Her non-violent philosophy still causes her to regard the Swede's way of life as a wasteland, but she is no longer polemical about it; simply, she will not return to it, and she never does.

The Swede sees both of Merry's personae as self-destructive, her present environment as revolting. He could not make sense of her actions in making bombs (she became an expert) even when he respected her opinions about the war. Now that she has given up violence, she lives in squalor in one room without light. Her bed, her clothes and her room are filthy, because she will not disturb any small organisms that might be harbouring there. She covers her face with a stocking to avoid hurting the inhabitants of the air. She is thin and does not stutter. The Swede thinks her way of living is a heavy price to pay for this. He cannot bear to think that she is worse off than one of Dawn's cows—there is an interesting parallel with the Prodigal Son story, but Merry does not come home repentant, as he does.

He warns her that the derelicts living in the underpass will harm her, which she denies. "They won't harm me. They know that I love them." For the Swede, however,

The words sickened him, the flagrant childishness, the sentimental grandiosity of the self-deception. What does she see in the hopeless scurryings of these wretched people that could justify such an idea? Derelicts and love? To be a derelict living in an underpass is to have clobbered out of you a hundred times over the minutest *susceptibility* to love. This was awful.

Merry lives in her wasteland for another 25 years, until she dies. Swede continues to visit her, unbeknownst to everyone except Jerry.

Dawn, who has shared the Swede's dream of colonial America come again, has never left it except to undergo severe depression as a result of being known as the mother of the Rimrock Bomber. In this period when she is hospitalized she relives her glory days at the Miss America pageant, and only comes out of her reverie of the past after an expensive and painful face-lift in Switzerland and the decision (hers alone) to build a new house. Swede is crushed by the idea, but believes that the old house must hold too many sad memories of Merry, so he agrees to sell the place he adores. At the dinner party, which is the final scene in the book, he discovers that Dawn and Bill Orcutt, the architect, are lovers. Moments after, he listens to Dawn telling another happy story about their trip to Europe to buy cattle years ago. She is rejuvenated but out of touch with the present: "Yes, if you'd missed her back in the forties, here once again was Mary Dawn Dwyer of Elizabeth's Elmora section...." As always, the Swede holds in his anger, and lets her build another dream world with Orcutt in the new house. He never tells her about Merry. Dawn sees no wasteland, except during the brief but miserable time in hospital, and she carries on trying to keep the fantasy of colonial America alive.

Hers is the kind of "creative amnesia" we find in the Exodus wilderness, where people grumbled about hardships, remembering only the food they had eaten in Egypt, and forgetting that they had been slaves forced to work under almost impossible conditions. In one instance this amnesia backfired vehemently. In the part of the journey that is called the "spy narrative," scouts were sent to find out what the land of Canaan was like, how bountiful it was, and how powerful its people. Many of them returned exaggerating the difficulties of conquering it and disparaging its fertility. They said that the inhabitants were so gigantic it made them feel like grasshoppers. They roused the whole community against

God for bringing them there, completely ignoring his promises to them, and finally he lost his temper with them, with dire results. All who had come into the wilderness, with a few exceptions, would die there, he said, never reaching the land he had given them. Those who had brought back the false information about Canaan were killed on the spot.

All of the Swede's family live out either an ideology or a fantasy, of what was past, is now, or is to come. Only the Swede is able to let the scales of think-kindly liberalism fall from his eyes. After the bomb that tosses him out of his perfect life in his shrine-like enclave into "the indigenous American berserk," he tries to find explanations for Merry's act, but, according to Jerry, this self-questioning comes too late. Eventually he realizes what Jerry has always known, that life makes no sense—"It is chaos. It is chaos from start to finish." Jerry concurs with his brother, who says that "what *anybody* is *is not enough*." "You got it!" he says. "Exactly! We are *not* enough. We are *none* of us enough! Including even the man who does everything right!"

When the last blow falls, as Dawn takes a lover and casts the Swede out of the picture, he sees himself as a "captive confined to a futureless box.... However much he might crave to get out, he was to remain stopped dead in the moment in that box. Otherwise the world would explode." This is the blackest moment in his life so far. What happens next we only discover in brief through Skip's conversations with him at their dinner meeting, and later with Jerry. During dinner the Swede had told Skip that he had a second wife and three boys—no mention of a daughter—and had just had a successful prostate operation. The real story is, according to Jerry, that wife number two is utterly selfish, and that the prostate operation didn't work, so he died. The Swede had stayed in a box for the rest of his life, trying all the while to build up a copy of the good life he once had, while torn apart with anguish, "a riven charlatan of sincerity."

The Swede has come into a wasteland that is made more cruel because of the fantasy pastoral he has left behind. He goes on with his life like Milton's Christ, with "the better fortitude/Of Patience and Heroic Martyrdom." Unlike Christ, however, he is unrewarded, and unlike Milton's Adam, having been cast out from Paradise, he does not achieve a "Paradise within thee, happier farr"[23] than the world he left behind. For the Swede there is no more sacred place or time; there is only the wasteland of meaninglessness and falsity; the prophet's prediction of a harsh wind from the desert that will destroy everything that has taken place.

At the last, very quietly, we find the narrator, Skip, lodged in what seems to be his own private wasteland. From the little he will tell us, the world as he once knew it has changed in two respects: his body is failing, and he cannot make sense of other people. This well-known writer lives alone in a small place in the woods with no one to talk to except the storekeeper and the postmistress. He has had a heart bypass, a cancer scare, and a prostate operation that has left him impotent and incontinent. He describes writing as a way of distancing himself from "the picture we have of one another. Layers and layers of misunderstanding. The picture we have of *ourselves*. Useless. Presumptuous. Completely cocked-up. Only we go ahead and we *live* by these pictures." It seems to the reader that Skip is in part writing his own story when he takes on the Swede's. Even his attempt to be philosophical about it fails him:

> The fact remains that getting people right is not what living is all about anyway. It's getting them wrong that is living, getting them wrong and wrong and wrong and then, on careful reconsideration, getting them wrong again. That's how we know we're alive: we're wrong. Maybe the best thing would be to forget being right or wrong about people and just go along for the ride. But if you can do that—well, lucky you.

Although life goes on in a rather ordinary way for Skip, with no violent intrusions—most of us have had failed love affairs and many get ill—the story behind his story seems remarkably like the Swede's. This may be the last word about the truth of the novel. Paradise is definitely lost. Welcome to the real world, the wasted land.

As I reread this great novel, I am bothered by the usual questions. In this tough-chewing bite of reality that Roth hands us, what went wrong, and what might have served us better (or, what might we have done better)? How did the American dream result in "the indigenous American berserk"? Perhaps too simplistically, I want to begin at the beginning, and lay the blame first on Genesis 1:28-29. God gives the man and the woman dominion over the other creatures, and he gives all the trees and plants to them for food. The emphasis that we have placed on this idea, that we can conquer everything we need, has been part of what theologian Elizabeth Johnson calls the master narrative of the West. Conquering and being conquered over the centuries because we "need" more land, more animals, more food, has been part of our game plan, supported by divine right. In America the Puritans tackled it afresh, taming the land while treating it as unimportant, even unholy. At the same time they looked on the barbarous local inhabitants as part and parcel of their directive to dominate. Edward Johnson wrote in 1654 of Jehovah's achievement over the previous 20 years in reducing the population of Massachusetts Indians from 30,000 to 300.

Max Weber has shown how the Puritan idea of rational business practice, coupled with the ethical requirement to squirrel away the proceeds to avoid ostentatious living, produced plenty of capital. As Puritanism lost ground, capitalism remained, and the notion of paradise within you or paradise to come became that of paradise on earth, visible, graspable. Immigration furthered the dream. Enter the Levovs along with everyone else.

Today the dream has turned into a nightmare for such as the Swede and Merry, and a blinkered fantasy to most of the rest of us, although thankfully not all. Elizabeth Johnson records Edward Farley's argument:

> No longer do the clear and distinct ideas of universal reason, the gains of unending progress, the supremacy of white, male culture supported by violence, and human domination over nature drive interpretation, but attention focuses on what is disruptive, ironic, contingent, different, ambiguous.[24]

I wonder, if the master narrative had not been derived from those lines from Genesis, would we have had a different society? If God had not evolved into a bad-tempered despot and had remained the mysterious, wise creator, how would we have turned out? Even Jesus' presentation of God came too late: Roman emperors in his time were gods/despots, too, and it was their image that was transferred to the symbolic kingdom called Christianity. In the next play, the despot comes to centre stage.

Samuel Beckett probably was the prophet of minimalism. No one can reduce the prerequisites of human life to such a tiny staged heap of artifacts employed by a little cast of grotesque yet ordinary people the way he can. No one can take such a small cargo of words and arm them fully with ironic, referential, symbolic meaning, in such a way that the word hoard seems to expand, not disappear. When you put all these ingredients together in *Endgame*—impoverished stage, incapacitated people, brittle, self-referential language—you get a wasteland as devastating as any in literature.

This wilderness, for all that its physical setting differs from the biblical, resembles it in its most desolate and cruel modes. It is the wilderness upon which God rains down curses, and which he threatens with worse. The two predominant features are its barrenness and its corruption of moral values. The stage setting is a colourless, bare room in an empty landscape. Inside the room the two curtained windows are too high up to see out. The painting has its face turned to the wall. At the start of the play three characters are hidden by sheets like furniture in a house whose owners have left.

A plot analysis of the play is impossible, because there is very little action at all, and the conclusion, such as it is, is ambiguous. There are four characters: Hamm, who is blind and seated in a wheelchair; Clov, stiff-legged and unable to sit down; and Nagg and Nell, Hamm's parents, legless, living in dustbins, and visible onstage by the will of Hamm, who tells Clov when to lift the covers off the bins. Actions are performed—Clov takes Hamm for a ride around the room, he brings Hamm his toy dog, he brings in a ladder and climbs it to look out the windows—but the actions have no consequences. The play begins with Hamm's removing the bloody handkerchief that covers his face; it ends with his replacing it. In this ruined wilderness, the few familiar objects and necessary pieces of equipment either disappear or are useless. Hamm's painkillers and Nagg's sweets run out; the gaff, a hook Hamm uses to move his chair, will not work. It is pointless to get the ladder to look at the landscape from both windows, because there is no difference between the view of the land on one side and the view of the sea—both are leaden and gray, and the light has sunk.

Except for the possibility that one or both of the parents have died quietly in their bins, matters seem to remain at a stalemate. Throughout the play the characters remark that the light is dying, everything is turning gray and indistinguishable from everything else, and all sources of nourishment and easement of pain have dried up. Yet it is difficult to believe that this play represents the end of the world. Clov threatens to leave Hamm, but has not done so; Hamm anticipates death, but has not died. In the performance I saw, there was no change in the light, inside or out.

(Do the characters lie, or are they deceived?) The last moment of the play looks precisely like the opening one. The meaning of what lies between the two is opaque.

Within the bare room are four maimed people who have exhibited all the familiar biblical vices—cruelty towards each other, abusive power, selfish lust in place of marital affection, refusal to respond to basic human needs and desires, murderous impulses (although no one is actually killed), pride, and duplicity. Their physical incapacities reinforce the notion that these relationships are based on mutual dependencies and nothing more. Nagg and Nell, with no legs, depend upon Hamm's whims for their food and cleanliness. Hamm can neither move nor see and depends upon Clov to carry out his orders. Because Clov can walk but not sit, he is given to perpetual motion. He is physically able to leave Hamm but will not. His dependence upon Hamm is more than physical.

The vicious natures of these characters and their mutual dependencies are exaggerated because they are distortions of family life. Nagg and Nell are Hamm's parents. Clov, Hamm implies, is his adopted son whom he treats as a servant, although there is an equality between them that comes from a mutually shared need. The need is to play a game together.

There are so many allusions within the play to other works and themes that I am tantalized by the urge to hunt them all out, but the play cannot be subdued by an attempt to integrate all of these, to reduce it to a set of ideas, no matter how complex. One great moving metaphor, that of the chess game, exposes and expands on our wilderness as a land now laid waste, through either human wickedness or divine wrath, or both.

The endgame is the series of inevitable moves, when one player knows he has lost, by which the chess game is concluded. Here is the beginning of the underlying ambiguity in the play. For Hamm and Clov are black pieces, Nagg and Nell white; yet they are not really opposed. Hamm needs Nagg in order to have an audience for the ongoing story he is spinning out. Although Hamm is the king piece, he is limited in his moves just as a king is in chess, but here it is his pawn who must move him about. At the same time Hamm abuses Clov—he has never given Clov a bicycle, and he will give him only enough food to keep him alive, he says. Nagg and Nell refuse help from each other when it is offered.

The sides are drawn up as though they were doing battle not against each other, but against something else.

The reason for this is that the characters don't know, and neither do we, whether they are players or pieces in this game. Hamm's authoritative "Me—to play" and "We're getting on" are countered by statements evoking passivity: "Something is taking its course." They may be pieces in some vaster game manipulated by something or someone else, or they may be players who are able to move within certain limits, but who are unable to end the game when they choose. The outcome seems not to be up to them, in either case, and it is not even clear that there is an outcome. What seems to be implied is that the characters are in part responsible for the way the game has been played, though perhaps not totally responsible.

The endgame is being played in the wilderness, and the two images together account for the connection with the biblical antecedents. For the endgame is, usually, the last part of a movement or journey towards a goal, the completion of the game. In this play, though, all the motion is circular, or forward and back, not unlike the travel of the Exodus wanderers. The wilderness of the Exodus is suggested here through references to manna, to shelter, to going into the desert, and, in the French version, to the little boy in the distance who looks as Moses did at the Promised Land. But this wilderness is far worse than that of the Exodus. Clov's seeds will not sprout, rain is needed but will not come, and the sawdust that had formerly lined the dustbins has now been replaced by sand, implying the loss of trees. Hamm dreams of forests that are no more. Even people will be reduced to heaps of sand, "a little bit of grit in the middle of the steppe." This is Hamm's vision, that the world will dissolve into a sandy, empty waste.

While the Exodus is implicit in this picture, Hamm sets the wilderness within the context of creation, with himself as first cause. What we have here is an image of devolution, of what has happened to the whole world since the expulsion from Eden. The history of the world is of a continual worsening and a continual journeying, yet there is no promised land at the end of the trip. The world has reached such a wasted state that the only outcome imaginable is the end of the game. Either the behaviour of the creature himself will end it, or perhaps the game is driven by an external, non-human player who will end it. No such person is alluded to, but the ambiguity about whether the characters are chess players or chess pieces suggests that not all responsibility may be laid at the door of humans.

The creation story is clearly parodied in the play. Hamm is the unmoved mover who holds the key to the food cupboard. Hamm says snidely to Clov, "You're a bit of all right, aren't you?" an ironic reference to God's observation that creation is totally all right. Clov replies, "A smithereen," and Hamm says, "This is slow work," compared to God's, which was instantaneous. Hamm says, "This is not much fun. But that's always the way at the end of the day, isn't it, Clov?" God, in contrast, was pleased at the end of each day.

This parody of God's behaviour changes, becomes confused, when Hamm says, "What's happening, what's happening?" and imagines a non-answer, "Something is taking its course." He cannot complete what he started: "Will this never finish?" The single flea he finds must be killed, because "humanity might start from there all over again." Still, Hamm has delusions of divine grandeur. His chair must be placed in the exact centre of the room; he must be taken "right round the world"; and he uses the royal "we." He says of Clov's lack of understanding, "Ah the creatures, the creatures, everything has to be explained to them." Both Hamm and Clov are obsessed with the idea of days, today, yesterday. Hamm asks Clov what yesterday means. "That means that bloody awful day, long ago, before this bloody awful day." When Hamm asks whether this "thing" has gone on long enough, and is told yes, he says, "Then it's a day like any other day," contradicting the idea that the days of creation were entirely different from each other. Here is Clov's notion of order: "I love order. It's my dream. A world where all would be silent and still and each thing in its last place, under the last dust." Order, then, is not the created order, but the annihilation of that.

Hamm is of course not God. He is crippled, blind, incontinent, cruel, and desperately confused. He no longer knows the difference between night and day. What power he has is used to destroy life, not to create it. He is a human being who has taken on godlike activity and has produced only a mess. He is the fruit of God's prediction in Genesis 3:23—he has become like a god—and in this play there is the hint that he has perhaps eaten from the tree of life and will live forever. The insinuation is that since the expulsion from Eden people have been in a wilderness that is self-caused and have achieved only distortions of the original Edenic idea.

Hamm sits in the centre of this mess, still playing out his godlike fantasy, but at the same time realizing that he is a man in part responsible. There is no God to intervene; man alone must finish the game, or make the attempt, since the way to end the game eludes him. The Exodus contract between God and the Hebrews is recalled in ironic inversion:

Hamm: You don't love me.
Clov: No.
Hamm: You loved me once.
Clov: Once!
Hamm: I've made you suffer too much.
(Pause)
Haven't I?

We watch the characters playing out the game using methods they know are meaningless. Hamm and Clov try to pray in vain; there is no reply. "The bastard!" Hamm cries. "He doesn't exist!" Beckett satirizes other methods that people have used to keep the meaning of the world intact. The certainty of a man's position at the centre of the room (read, the universe?) is established by a blind man guessing. Clov's mathematically punctilious movements to look at the landscape are rewarded by just what he expected: nothing but grayness. "All is corpsed."

Four different views of nature are implicit in the following dialogue:

Hamm: Nature has forgotten us.
Clov: There's no more nature.
Hamm: No more nature! You exaggerate.
Clov: In the vicinity.
Hamm: But we breathe, we change! We lose our hair,
    our teeth! Our bloom! Our ideals!
Clov: Then she hasn't forgotten us.

The exchange concludes with Clov saying, "No one that ever lived ever thought so crooked as we," implying that they do not believe any of the points of view they have been declaiming. In the theatre, I listened to, and joined in with, the knowing laughter that Beckett's ironic tongue brings out. As the play went on, the laughter was drained of the chuckle element and became a faint snicker. No more jokes, just a grow-ing unease.

As everything in the world erodes, so does language. In response to a question about the meaning of "yesterday," Clov says, "I use the words you taught me. If they don't mean anything any more, teach me oth-ers"—another reference to the creation story. Speech is pointless, its only meaning ritualistic. "I love the old questions. Ah the old questions, the old answers, there's nothing like them!" says Hamm. The erosion of meaning and of the old answers, however, is evident from the first line of the play: "Finished, it's finished, nearly finished, it must be nearly finished." That "it" may not be nearly finished is suggested by Hamm's refrain, "Old endgame lost of old, play and lose and have done with losing." That "it" should finish is the characters' desire: the most appall-ing question of all is, "We're not beginning to...to...mean something?" The idea strikes Hamm and Clov as absurd.

The loss of humanness and the loss of meaning go hand in hand, and it is never clear to what extent the characters themselves contribute to the annihilation of both. When Clov asks, "Do you believe in the life to come?" Hamm replies, "Mine was always that." If there was a prom-ised land ahead, he won't get there. He has come into the cosmic situa-tion during the endgame: "Absent, always. It all happened without me. I don't know what's happened." Yet they seem to have a choice. Clov: "Let's stop playing." Hamm: "Never!" And the last speech of Hamm's is that of a man acting out a part to the end, thus giving the twist to the sense of reality that has been built up thus far. Player or piece is still undecided, as is the extent and ownership of the board.

One might visualize a wasteland as having nothing in it whatsoever. Imaginatively Beckett has surpassed that idea, because the recorded ab-sence or uselessness of things heightens the sense of loss, of the strip-ping of nature of all order, all sustenance, all beauty and all pleasure. Introducing a toy dog that has three legs and cannot stand up is a far more powerful way to show the bleakness of Hamm's relationships than not to mention any creature at all. Hamm asks to be wheeled right round the world, which is his room; had he said right round the room, there would be no sense of the world as the wilderness reduced to his room. The bloody handkerchief over Hamm's face points beyond itself to the remains of a human being underneath it. Because the question of who the players really are in this game of life is never answered, the wilderness stands out as the overarching absence, the image that remains after everything else has gone. We are left here with an experience bereft of a context of meaning, bereft of hope, and with the threat that the game may be repeatable, the sordid wilderness an endless possibility.

These are not people who think about the wilderness from a distance, or who travel through it with the hope of emerging finally in the land of promise, or who have escaped into it from an oppressive city, or who are being punished there for a limited time. They are there because there is no other place, and are well aware, unlike the dwellers in Jerusalem or Babylon, that it is a wilderness. They experience it as their whole world. Whether they have been set up or not, it is their cruelty, their indifference, their refusal of love, that make it such.

7

— THE INTERIOR WILDERNESS —

With a heart of furious fancies,
Whereof I am commander;
With a burning spear,
And a horse of air,
To the wilderness I wander.

Anonymous, "Tom o' Bedlam"

Be calm but vigilant, because your enemy the devil is prowling around like a roaring
lion, looking for someone to eat.

1 Peter 5:8

For nothing can be sole or whole
That has not been rent.

W.B. Yeats, "Crazy Jane talks with the Bishop"

Going mad is what you do in the North.

Margaret Atwood, *Strange Things: The Malevolent North*
in Canadian Literature

I f the wilderness hasn't crept into your mind by this time, then I've missed my mark in the telling of how these writings work on us. For wherever you find a starkly compelling wilderness, it will be haunted by an uneasy traveller. Landscape and inscape belong together, each calling to each. I can hardly separate Inman's sadly quizzical mind from the dreary, poisoned terrain he wanders. Pierre's lonely questing is kith and kin to the hiddenness of Ungava. Gregor's forest protects and allows him to discover what freedom is now open to him.

I do wonder to what extent landscape determines who you are. Here's a melodramatic example of what I mean, in fiction and real time. When we bought an old village house in France, our version of a summer cottage, we called it "Colomba," after the heroine of Merimée's book. It was a novel I remembered from my university days, in which a handsome, courageous, impatient Corsican woman attempts to avenge her father's murder, with disastrous results. From Merimée I learned about the Corsican eye-for-an-eye blood feud called the vendetta, a practice that continued in the nineteenth century. It seemed inconceivable that this sort of tribal warfare could have gone on so late in what we think of as the most civilized continent in the world.

After 17 years of living under "Colomba's" roof, we decided one year to seek out our adopted origins, and go to Corsica. We rented part of a house in a village not far from Fozzano, where the real Colomba had lived, and very much liked it. While most people go to Corsica for its gorgeous white, curving beaches, the interior of the island, particularly in the south, is ragged with mountains. Their silhouettes are at times low, heavy mounds; in other places they are slim, quizzically formed, as if some giant was running out of clay and stuck bits on top and sides just to finish off. Boulders with hollowed-out centres, hooked sides, and smooth tops act as protective devices against anyone bold enough to climb there. We found several of these that had been used as dwellings by Bronze Age settlers. Everywhere the mountains and the valleys between are covered with *maquis*, a dense, low-growing shrub, its gray-blue leaves offering no depth or variation of colour. It is as it looks, a tough surface disguising the even tougher rock of the mountains themselves.

Set in this bold landscape are the little mountain villages that over the centuries have continued to fight with each other. To a stranger such as myself, the idea of making this cruel and unusual setting even more so by toughing it out against each other, instead of against the landscape, seems absurd, but that's what Corsican families did. The vendetta seems to have died out now, but my guidebook says that the last person to have avenged his family's honour by murder died about 15 years ago, at age 90!

Colomba's village, like the one we are staying in, is lovely in the sunlight with all the wildflowers blooming beside the road, vibrant rose and yellow-centred white cystis growing in abundance down the hill-sides, wistaria tumbling over and between the intricate iron tracery of the balconies on every house overlooking the street—except two. Two stone towers, bleak and unadorned, overlook Fozzano, where the two leading families lived, and from which they descended to kill each other in the main square, on the road outside the village, or in the *maquis*. Colomba's family was one of these. Although the vendetta is over, and the people whose voices we heard as we traipsed along the streets sounded as cheery as market day, the village obviously still lives in part in the old memory, so helpfully kept alive by Merimée. It isn't hard to do; all you have to do is look at the surroundings. This is true wilderness, a place where the physical presence of the landscape can surely be sister to the emotional savagery of its past inhabitants, if not its instigator. I've never felt so much a stranger as here. I have also read that the real Colomba was an ugly, ferocious, irrational old woman. She and her tower are a believable adjunct to this difficult and unruly region.

Landscape does more than affect your mood. It attacks you in the inner place. A savage or wasted place can act upon you to disturb your equilibrium; or, in reverse, the unsettled mind can turn an uninhabited country into a ghastly domain. What then are we to make of Hamm and his world? Is he the blind king, the cause of his land's sickness? Or is he the unmoved chess piece, the victim of a vicious game, where the board itself is in disarray? Or are the two, person and world/board, in cahoots—we might say homologous, in a nonjudgmental way, but I think cahoots has the right flavour for the work. If both are sick, mad, or bad, then on what ground, what common platform, do we stand in order to say so?

What can we say of Merry's or Vico's or Cristina's position vis-à-vis their blasted worlds? Are they wrong to act as they do, or are they mad? (Don't think that they are all in the same boat, or behave in the same way for the same reasons. They are, if nothing else, outsiders in a wilderness, partly self-chosen, partly thrust upon them.) Madness is the thread that is beginning to appear through many of these wilderness tales—at least I think it is, depending on how you define it. You could say, simply, that madness is what society says it is. Anyone who is out of order, a disturber of our peace, if she or he goes far enough, is mad. But what if in the end our society is condemned as mad or bad by another authority? Then these madmen are rehabilitated and it is we, the society, who are out of order. I remember when the first tree-huggers were thought to be loony, when Greenpeace was definitely anti-social. Now we are outraged when our politicians do not save our swamps and forests and when they fail to build in policies to preserve our endangered species.

Perhaps, without trying to find the high moral ground, I might say that a person is mad who, although capable of answering skill-testing questions, is driven in one direction incessantly, propelled by overpowering, often conflicting emotions. Madness and wildness are both conditions of derangement, of being out of order. Then it's only a question of degree: how far out of order must you be to be mad? How disordered must a society be in order to be thought a wilderness, a place run by the insane? And who or what says so?

It may seem strange to turn to the Bible for examples of madness. Biblical writings do not explore individual character traits or describe personalities. Such ideas have not come into their own time yet. Yet you can imagine how some of the dramatis personae might be, just hearing their words and knowing their undertakings. Think of John the Baptist: can you imagine him as a contemporary priest, or a social worker, or even a Tai Chi instructor or a gospel singer? He is too elusive for that, too indifferent to all but his proclamation, too unkempt, too hairy. On Yonge Street we would take him for one of the homeless ones; in the country we'd see a tramp and call the cops. Above all, we'd think him mad. Just stand him at Eaton's beside Santa Claus and listen to both voices. You'd know.

Take a look at Moses' life. It's a series of shocks, revelations, impossible demands. It outclasses Grisham or le Carré in the number and gravity of unwarranted knocks and eruptions of ordinary life. In fact, Moses has no ordinary life at all. Stolen from his birth mother and brought up as a foreign princess' son, gold spoon and all, at some point he realizes he is nothing but a slave's child. As a young adult, trying to rescue one of his people, he kills an Egyptian and escapes to the wilderness, knowing even his adoptive royal mum can't help him. Nor would he want her to. Here is where his life changes: in the wilderness he is charged by God with rescuing the Hebrews from slavery. To go once to his step-granddad the Pharaoh with an economically ridiculous request (let your free labour force go) would have been hard enough. To threaten said Pharaoh with stunning retribution was suicide. To do this seven times...can we not call this a kind of madness shared only by dictators and gurus? God, it seems, prefers madmen. What should we deduce from that?

I wonder how some of those fiery, bile-in-their-throat prophets—Jeremiah, Elijah, Ezekiel, Amos—were treated by their unwilling audiences. Were they thought to be demoniacs whose spirits should be driven into the swine? Or were they just ignored as grumpy old men? The compilers of the Hebrew Bible thought they were holy, not insane.

There are some literary worlds that I do not really want to step into. I'm never sure exactly why. Sometimes I think it's a question of mood. Or perhaps it's the strangeness of the writer's approach—I meet a gravelly tone when I am expecting sympathy. Sometimes the world being described is just too ugly, too rough, more like my nightmares than my utopian fantasies. So I hesitate, and often just turn away and look for a more acceptable vision. Most of the time, though, when I do keep on going down the road the author has pointed out, I find myself captivated willy-nilly by the very presence of that world. Its grimness is there, but it has been changed in the telling. An author worth the reading doesn't just rub my nose in others' dirt, others' blues. She helps me to make sense of her literary world, and then my everyday one, even if it's to claim that the world, the big real one, makes no sense at all.

What is it about Flannery O'Connor's novel *The Violent Bear It Away* that sets up in me a mixture of dread, dislike, and admiration? For one thing, I think that for reasons I can't fathom yet, it is very close to the bone. The book makes me fidget and squirm, pull back, and then throw myself into it again, I know not why. I'll think about this, but not yet.

If you ever thought you really knew what madness is, consider this novel carefully. If you have settled for a wilderness you can live with, in life or fiction, now look at this one. That is the quiddity of madness and wilderness, that they are elusive, shifting, tricky, and dangerous to know. In this novel the characters know that, and we come to see it, too. The story begins in one wilderness—the isolated countryside—and ends in another—the dissolute city. O'Connor does not pose one against the other in a moral sense; each takes on different colouring depending on which character sees it. For the wilderness dweller, the city is a challenge to be taken up; for the city dweller, the wilderness is haunted with bad memories. In one place or another, the wilderness is where you meet your opponents, wild beasts and devils.

This is a New Testament story with Old Testament fury. While the subject is a Christian one, the voices ring out with the shrillness of the ancient prophets declaiming against the world's iniquities. Perhaps we'll find some New Testament fury in it, too. Although there are three main characters, there are actually only two voices: the devil and the good Lord.

The oddly assorted group is made up of three generations from one family. There is Mason Tarwater, who is uncle to George Rayber, who is in turn uncle to Francis Tarwater. Mason has taken young Tarwater away from Rayber to live with him in his shack in a clearing in the woods a mile off a dirt road. There he is teaching him everything he needs to know in order to become his successor as a prophet. This modern Elijah and his reluctant Elisha eke out their existence by planting corn and eating berries and fish. Mason wears the clothes he intends to be buried in.

Rayber is a schoolteacher who, when he was seven years old, was kidnapped by Mason and taken to the shack to live with him and, first and foremost, to be baptized. After four days his father took him home, despite the boy's pleas to stay. Years later, Rayber returns to the shack to curse his uncle for having ruined his life, and to shriek at him that he is mad. Now Rayber himself has a son, Bishop, who is feeble-minded and does not speak. Mason is determined that he shall be baptized. Rayber is equally determined that he shall not be.

Mason is every inch a prophet. He has been "burned clean and burned clean again." The second time this happened, it signified that he was not to proclaim "the destruction awaiting a world that had abandoned its Saviour." He now knew "it was saving and not destruction he was seeking." He was waiting for the call to save Bishop by baptizing him, but should it not come, then it would be Tarwater's job.

His opinion of his nephew Rayber is scathingly assured. Years ago Mason had lived in the city with him for three months, and all the while that Rayber was questioning him keenly about his calling and his early life, he was secretly putting it all down in an article in a "schoolteacher magazine." He wrote about Mason's "fixation" about being called, about his childhood insecurity, as a result of which, Rayber says, he had called himself. Enraged that Rayber had been "creeping into his soul by the back door," Mason took Tarwater from his crib and hightailed it to the wilderness.

Tarwater is quite taken with the idea of being a prophet like Joshua or Daniel, a profession with a lot of drama and excitement to it. He has been to the city and sees that it is evil. "He saw in a burst of light that these people were hastening away from the Lord God Almighty. It was to the city that the prophets came and he was here in the midst of it." In his fantasy about being a prophet, he expects "to see wheels of fire in the eyes of unearthly beasts." He is less enthusiastic when his uncle speaks of hungering for the bread of life that is Jesus. He doesn't want anything to do with "this threatened intimacy of creation" and is afraid that some day "he would be torn by hunger like the old man, the bottom split out of his stomach so that nothing would heal or fill it but the bread of life."

With Mason's death, matters come to a head. Tarwater is under orders from the old man to dig him a deep hole for a grave, but the ground is hard and he stops to drink some alcohol from the old man's still and falls asleep. On waking, he decides to do what Mason had said the schoolteacher would have done, by setting fire to the shack in which Mason has died. Then he goes to town to tell Rayber what he has done, and moves in with him.

Enter the voice of "liberated" reason. Rayber believes that Tarwater has been corrupted by Mason and promises to change all that. As he says, "getting out from under the old man is just like coming out of the darkness into the light"—a metaphor that he probably does not recognize as biblical. What neither of them realizes is the inner wrenching and resisting that this situation sets up for them both.

While Mason is a modern revival of a biblical prophet, with no doubt whatever about his calling, the other two characters are seething emotional vessels stirred by the opposing forces of God and the devil. In Tarwater the opposition is clear. He is sliced into two personae: the self who has been instructed by Mason, and the strange voice that emerges after Mason's death. At first the stranger's voice seems loud and disagreeable. Gradually he becomes Tarwater's persuasive friend, who advises him that to be a prophet is to be lost forever, and that there is no devil, only a choice between Jesus or his own self. Tarwater swings wildly between his two "selves." He follows Mason's orders and baptizes Bishop by holding him under in the lake until he drowns. Immediately after-wards he internalizes the friend's voice, rationalizing that the baptism was only an accident, the drowning intentional. Abandoning Mason's directive, he intends to go home and "make good his refusal" to be a prophet. He heads for Mason's shack, egged on by the "friend" who says, "Go down and take it.... It's ours. We've won it." Yet in this mo-ment something changes within Tarwater, and he shudders. He feels—here is as good a description of the devil as I've ever read—that "The presence was as pervasive as an odor, a warm sweet body of air encir-cling him, a violent shadow hanging around his shoulders." At the same time, he is struck by "a hunger too great to be contained inside him." He sets fire to the bushes and trees on the homestead, making "a rising wall of fire between him and the grinning presence. He glared through the flames and his spirits rose as he saw that his adversary would soon be consumed in a roaring blaze." Afterwards, looking across at the field, Tarwater has a vision in which he becomes "aware of the object of his hunger, aware that it was the same as the old man's and that nothing on earth would fill him." Mason (and God) have won after all.

Rayber's anguish, on the other hand, comes from unbidden erup-tions of emotion into a withered life that excludes the pain of love and the pleasures of the senses, and filters all experience through his mind. He has rejected the salvation that Mason made possible by baptizing him, and believes that "there's no saviour but yourself." From time to time, no matter how he tries to prevent it, he is overwhelmed by "horri-fying love," of Bishop, or of any simple thing: "If, without thinking, he lent himself to it, he would feel suddenly a morbid surge of the love that terrified him—powerful enough to throw him to the ground in an act of idiot praise." If I didn't know better, I would think this was a prophet speaking of his call. It is, however, Rayber, who calls the experience irrational. He recognizes his struggle as being between madness and emptiness, and he forces himself to choose the latter. He knows that if he were to lose Bishop he would be confronted with the world to love, and that he would have to resist with all his might, to "anesthetize his life." Yet the struggle persists, as "a sinister pull on his consciousness, the familiar undertow of expectation, as if he were still a child waiting on Christ." When he realizes that Bishop has been drowned, he hears bel-lowing sounds that "seem to come from inside him as if something in him were tearing itself free." Then he stands, "waiting for the raging pain, the intolerable hurt that was his due, to begin, so that he could ignore it, but he continued to feel nothing." The last we hear of Rayber is that he collapses. Whatever life is left to him is no life at all.

Flannery O'Connor has done her homework. In choosing the title, she has presented us with a riddle, as one biblical scholar calls it, and left us to solve it through reading her novel. The title is a conundrum, which irked me because I couldn't see how it was meant to help me understand the work. It almost seemed to go against the drift. O'Connor is using part of a verse from Matthew 11. She quotes the whole verse as an epigraph: "From the days of John the Baptist until now, the kingdom of heaven suffereth violence, and the violent bear it away."

What does this phrase mean? I searched for a different translation of the text that would help explain. The RSV, the Jerusalem Bible, even Crossan's use of the text, are all like O'Connor's. J.B. Phillips has an unusual take on it; he translates, "From the days of John the Baptist until now the kingdom of Heaven has been taken by storm and eager men are forcing their way into it." Does this mean that the only way to enter heaven is through violence? That it is barricaded against all those desiring people, who must beat down the gates to get in?

A possible solution to the riddle comes from Joachim Jeremias, who finds it in an article by another New Testament scholar, F.W. Danker. He says that Jesus is speaking about his followers as they are viewed by the Jewish establishment, as opponents: "these sinners who follow Jesus force their way into the holy precincts reserved for the pious. They are...'violent intruders'"[25] There's an ironic sense to this that suits me, but is it what Jesus really meant? It certainly fits well with the tone of the earlier part of this chapter, when Jesus asks people about John the Baptist: "So what did you expect to find in the wilderness, someone wearing fine clothes?"

In fact, *The Violent Bear It Away* is almost a beautifully crafted gloss on the whole of Matthew 11. For instance, when John asks Jesus if he is the promised Messiah, the reply is, see what I have done—healing, cleansing and preaching to the poor. In a similar manner, Tarwater says to Rayber, "All you can do is think what you would have done if you had done it. Not me. I can do it. I can act." Then he takes Bishop out, baptizes him to suit his great-uncle, drowns him to satisfy his uncle. John the Baptist and Mason have much in common. John has the quintessential prophet's one-track mind. Both deliver similar messages to the people about salvation. Both are thought to be mad.

Now if you look at Tarwater and his great-uncle, outsiders, throwbacks, wild unsocialized men, and realize that it is they who will enter the kingdom, you catch the measure of what O'Connor is saying. She takes the same tack as the Jesus Matthew portrays, who thanks his father "for hiding these things from the learned and the clever and revealing them to mere children." O'Connor's own interpretation of her title comes from Thomas Aquinas: "The violent are not natural. St. Thomas's gloss on this verse is that the violent Christ is here talking about represent those ascetics who strain against mere nature. St. Augustine concurs."[26] The violent are mad for God; they are, in a way, supernatural.

This book is about the wilderness of testing and of temptation. Temptation and being called go together. O'Connor leads us quite directly to think about Jesus' temptation following his baptism. The devil tempts Jesus to want to know everything possible, to let himself go and tempt God to help him, to worship him. O'Connor's devil says you can be free, be yourself, let your reason guide you, know everything. Following his rejection of the devil, Jesus takes up his calling and begins to preach. Here is the conclusion of Tarwater's story:

> He felt his hunger no longer as a pain but as a tide. He felt it rising in himself through time and darkness, rising through the centuries, and he knew it rose in a line of men whose lives were chosen to sustain it, who would wander in the world, strangers from that violent country where the silence is never broken except to shout the truth.
>
> . . .
>
> He heard the command, GO WARN THE CHILDREN OF GOD OF THE TERRIBLE SPEED OF MERCY.
>
> . . .
>
> His singed eyes, black in their deep sockets, seemed already to envision the fate that awaited him but he moved steadily on, his face set toward the dark city, where the children of God lay sleeping.

O'Connor has roused the elements of fire and water in the wilderness to sustain the violent in their attack upon the kingdom.

Margaret Atwood knows a lot about the wilderness, and nowhere does she show it better than in *Surfacing*, one of her earliest novels. In this densely constructed novel you can find almost every strand of the biblical symbol of the wilderness, plus a contemporary update that would make the ancient prophets growl and nod grimly in agreement. In including the novel in this chapter, I am following Atwood's lead and highlighting her dominant theme, the anatomy of the mind as wilderness.

Here we are looking at a construction of madness different from O'Connor's, one that I saw in *The Snake Pit*, and the 1960s novel *I Never Promised You a Rose Garden*, among others. This madness, which usually finds people shut up in institutions (in the West, at least), is the state in which people construct a fantasy world in order to avoid the dangers they have felt in the everyday world, the one they have escaped from. Bringing them back into the "real" world is the therapists' job; some people never return, as it's safer to live in one's own private place. Some people are caught between their two worlds, surviving, but no more than that.

Atwood's heroine/narrator is one of these. *Surfacing* is the self-told story of the regeneration of a woman from a state of emotional paralysis and amnesia to her natural human condition. The story in brief: the narrator, who is never named, returns to the cabin on an island in the Quebec woods where she had spent part of her youth. She has been told that her father, living there alone, has disappeared. With her two best friends from the city (David and Anna) and her lover, Joe, she spends several days looking for him. Certain that he is alive, perhaps mad, she follows the clue she thinks he has left her in drawings he made of paintings on rock walls in the lake, dives into the lake to look for them, and has a terrifying vision. As a result of this, she hides on the island when it is time to leave with the others, staying alone and gradually adapting the habits and life of an animal. This phase is completed by a vision of her parents which, when it disappears, leaves her to begin her return to the life of a human being in civilization.

This summary must seem mystifying, a bit loony itself. What gives it sense is the other story, the one that unravels in the heroine's mind.

She has constructed a false history for her adult self that includes a marriage and a miscarriage. What she is hiding from her present self is that it was an affair with a married man, which resulted in a pregnancy that ended with an abortion. She reunites herself with her true memory when she dives into the water and sees a vision of "a dark oval trailing limbs...a dead thing." The rest of her story is her way of recovering from her past, of integrating her whole self: head, heart, and history.

Surfacing uses the literary structure of the voyage home to frame the story, but unlike *Cold Mountain*, it is not the voyage but the arrival that matters. The story begins with the heroine's return to the lakeside town from which she and her friends will take a boat to the cabin, a town where she has always felt an alien, "home ground, foreign territory." Now, so many years later, even the once familiar has been made strange. She feels cheated that there is a new, smooth road into town so she will not be carsick; mildly angry—she says betrayed—that her father's friend Paul's wife has replaced her wood stove with an electric one; and morally indignant to find her dead mother's jacket still on the hook: "Dead people's clothes ought to be buried with them." But the strangest change is the absence of her father, leaving an unweeded garden, a house that doesn't look lived in, and a puzzle as to his whereabouts. At first she is angry at him for leaving mysteriously, then frightened when she decides that he has become insane and may be lurking around the cabin "like a huge ragged moth." Later, she can't remember what she felt when she decided that he is both sane and dead—"Relief, grief," she thinks. "I must have felt one or the other." This is the ultimate estrangement: she cannot even picture his face. "He was as absent now as a number," she says, "a zero, the question mark in place of the missing answer." To overcome this estrangement she looks for a message from him, and eventually comes to discover the vision underwater that brings her back on the road to full life.

Although most of her emotional valves have been shut off, the narrator's ability to perceive and to learn is running at full strength. In watching her friends' behaviour in the bush, she comes to see her old surroundings and her new relationships in a different light, to re-evaluate the present and to refuse to acquiesce in the attitudes she abhors. We see first how city slickers treat the wilderness, and then how a wilderness-raised person sees the city. We realize, as we see the narrator reject David and Anna, that Jezebel and Elijah can never bear one another.

At first the narrator only notices the ineptness of the three city-bred people and their naïveté about the north. David's idea of the area is of "a marginal economy and grizzled elderly men," Anna wears the wrong clothes, neither of the men can steer the canoe, and both are clumsy with an axe. They all treat the excursion as a game, a hilarious adventure in getting back to nature—although they fill up the time with city pastimes, dialling stations on the radio, reading paperbacks, and playing cards. The holiday notion wears off quickly, as they chop only one log, fill half a cup with blueberries, and tire easily of weeding the garden. The country for them is just the city transferred: "A little beer, a little pot, some jokes, a little political chitchat, the golden mean; we're the new bourgeoisie, this might as well be a Rec Room."

The narrator's comments gradually hint at another view of the city dwellers. David "tatters and bends" trees. The log they chop for firewood ends up being "notched in many places as though they'd attacked it." It is more and more apparent that nature is for them the object of ridicule, despoliation, or indifference. Anna's songs are all ironic diminutions of the natural: "Mockingbird Hill," "You Are My Sunshine," "The Big Rock Candy Mountain." David and Joe have themselves filmed with the log they have butchered, "arms folded and one foot on it as if it was a lion or a rhinoceros." David's verbal violation of nature is linked with his sexual innuendoes and frequent comments about defecation.

On their canoe trip they find a dead heron strung up by its feet on a rope looped over a branch. The heroine moans and chastises herself for not having removed it, and becomes furious at "the Americans" who have caught it for sport and to prove their own prowess, as it is no use for food or anything else. The others look at the mangled bird as content for the film they are making: "It looks so great, you have to admit."

As their attitude to nature is unfolded, so is the failure of their personal lives. The key words to describe both are falsity and violation, through indifference, criticism, or direct aggression. In the narrator's eyes David is false through and through, "an imposter, a pastiche, layers of political handbills, pages from magazines, *affiches*, verbs and nouns glued on to him and shredding away, the original surface littered with fragments and tatters." Anna is "a seamed and folded imitation of a magazine picture that is itself an imitation of a woman who is also an imitation, the original nowhere, hairless lobed angel in the same heaven where God is a circle, captive princess in someone's head."

For David and Anna there is no hope. Joe, however, grows in the bush, from resembling a buffalo "threatened with extinction" to a person like the narrator who is barely born. He is also an animal who "needs to grow more fur," who, she thinks, is "only half-formed, and for that reason I can trust him."

The heroine's greatest fury is saved for those she calls "the Americans." They are those fishermen, friendly as sharks, who rob the waters of all the fish, stealing more than their quota, trampling ferns and plants, thrashing through the woods, and driving loons to death by gunning their powerboats behind them. Here are the heron killers: "Raygun fishing rods, faces impermeable as space-suit helmets, sniper eyes, they did it; guilt glittered on them like tinfoil." Gradually it dawns on the heroine that "American" is a name that belongs to people with a certain attitude towards the natural, not an epithet for a particular national group. The heron-killers are actually Canadians. "Americans" are people whose heads are developing metal where flesh was. They are becoming machines: "They are evolving, they are halfway to machine, the leftover flesh atrophied and diseased, porous like an appendix." They send electronic signals to each other: "They talk in numbers, the voice of reason."

Under the American umbrella are included those who were responsible for her abortion—her married lover and the people who performed the operation. Her lover tells her that the baby is not human, only an animal. Animals, in the "American" view, have no right to life. The operation was a metallic nightmare. She believes that she has had an animal inside her in a burrow and that she has let the Americans trap it. An "American," for her, is a victimizer, just as David and Anna are to each other, even to Joe. They "are already turning to metal, skins galvanizing, heads congealing to brass knobs, components and intricate wires ripening inside."

These people—David, Anna, the callous fishermen and medical operatives—are wastelanders, like those censured by the prophets for a list of similar sins. In this updated condemnation, the objectification of the human, the destruction of the natural for greed and for the mindless fun of it, have replaced apostasy, but the root of it all is the same: a desire to control what should instead be held in reverence and cherished.

Now that she can recognize and reject the Americans, the narrator is able to resolve, "above all, to refuse to be a victim. Unless I can do that," she thinks, "I can do nothing. I have to recant, give up the old belief that I am powerless and because of it nothing I can do will ever hurt anyone." This is the beginning of her regeneration, and her return to the city.

In this novel the wilderness is both agent and essence. It is abused by those who despoil or ridicule it. It is feared by the narrator, with the appropriate apprehension of a seasoned northerner who knows that the wilderness is a dangerous place. On top of this is her terror that her mad father will break in on them and her sense of being trapped on the island. As she undergoes her initiation into animal life, nature no longer seems vaguely fearful, but powerful in a controlling and guiding way. With her parents' disappearance, she comes to a true vision of nature as the harmonious interaction of humans with all of life. "The lake is quiet, the trees surround me, asking and giving nothing." Nature, like her, is to be neither victim nor victor, but simply itself.

In *Surfacing*, three narrative structures bring about the regeneration of the heroine: two employed by the woman herself, one by the author. The narrator undergoes a process in which memory, right judgment, emotions, and courage are restored to her, and in which fear, denial, transference, and myopia are exorcized. To do this, narrative forms of religious cult, psychological fantasy, and a familiar literary structure help to reinstate the needed qualities and bring down the barriers to real living.

In chronological order, the heroine, diving from her boat at one of the places sacred to the First Nations people, confronts underwater her taboo object, is suffused by fear, and surfaces, after which she recognizes the lie she has been living with respect to her aborted child. Filled with gratitude for the discovery, she leaves her offering to the gods, a sweatshirt, on the rock, as is customary, she says. This death and rebirth scenario is repeated in a different form when she takes Joe outside to have intercourse on the ground. The notion that sexual fertility and the fertility of the land are sympathetically related is the positive side of the Maimed King's story and a common idea in agricultural societies, where women and men have intercourse on the newly sown fields. The next day Atwood's narrator alone begins a lengthy and rigorous initiation rite, first burning and destroying all the civilizing props she has been used to—china, her old drawings, her sketches for her career as an illustrator, her clothes. She begins to receive guidance from her parents, who by degrees impose sanctions upon her with regard to shelter, enclosures, food—anything that is built or cultivated. In the end she makes a shelter of branches for herself, eats mushrooms and berries, and covers herself in a blanket, her only concession until she can grow fur. The withdrawal to the woods, the fasting, and the waiting for divine guidance are typical of First Nations initiation rituals. Finally, she has two hierophanies: one of her mother feeding the birds and turning into a jay herself; the other of her father, who changes shape from the "antlered fish thing" of the rock drawing to a fish in the lake. This concludes her phase of cultic behaviour; the gods-qua-parents have retired and she is free to do as she pleases.

What begins as a search for her father, and then for a message from him, has become an initiation rite, a hierophany, an exorcism, and a fertility ceremony. At last, after seeking guidance from her dead parents, they vanish, and the cultic ceremonies are over. She is alone in a world newly constructed in which there are no gods to help, no further messages from parents. She has received and felt the withdrawal of the *mana*-like power from the nature gods; now, the power is in herself—not magical, but appropriated to herself through her experiences.

In *Surfacing* the narrator uses psychological fantasy, at first in a negative, self-reducing way, and later as a way of reconnecting with herself and her world. When we meet her she has rewritten her past in order to reduce the pain of the actual past. We do not know this at first; she tells her story as true history, and except for a few hints that the story is confused, the reader doesn't know it is a fantasy until the woman herself discovers it. There is a tiny window that lets us glimpse this cover-up, in the description of the supposed wedding, which is actually the abortion episode. She has memories of the smell of antiseptic, of carrying a suitcase to the "post office" where the wedding took place, and of her "husband" talking to her "as though," she says, "I was an invalid, not a bride." But these clues don't emerge into full daylight to correct the fantasy until the moment of her underwater dive. After that, one can reread the earlier part of the book to recognize other pieces of the fantasy.

In the last sections of the book the narrator acts out a new fantasy, not only stripping herself of her own past, but simulating a natural regression from human to animal to plant form. The first form she is "forbidden" to take is her old persona: she may not look in the mirror. Next she must rid herself of all civilizing effects, by staying out of the enclosure and off the dock, by burning her drawings. In the third stage she becomes an animal, forbidden to enter the cabin, and required to forage in the garden for food. "The outhouse is forbidden," she thinks to herself, "so I leave my dung, droppings, on the ground and kick earth over. All animals with dens do that." Finally, with the garden out of bounds, she becomes a part of plant life: "I lean against a tree, I am a tree leaning." "I am not an animal or a tree, I am the thing in which the trees and animals move and grow. I am a place." The fantasy ends after she has seen her mother and father transformed into bird and fish and recognizes that "they have gone finally, back into the earth, the air, the water, wherever they were when I summoned them. The rules are over." She is now a natural woman. She says, "I re-enter my own time."

The mind's wilderness is caused by being split off from the rest of the body, sensational and emotional. The narrator says, "At some point my neck must have closed over, pond freezing or a wound, shutting me into my head." Half of her has been glassed in like "frogs in the jam jar stretched wide...." Even in her split existence, she connects herself metaphorically to the rest of nature. As we have seen, the action of the wilderness on her begins the process of reuniting the parts of herself, and herself with her environment. She is redeemable—unlike Rayber, whose fear is causing the rest of his emotional side to atrophy as he clings to the dried-up shreds of a rational life. Yet I find this heroine too cool to connect with; Rayber, in his tortured denials, is a livelier being. In *Surfacing* I watch and admire the process of coming to life; in *The Violent Bear It Away*, I draw back aghast in a kind of fear and trembling. Nothing changes: the devil was always more interesting, in literature if not in life.

Although I don't find the heroine emotionally compelling, the story has captivated me, because in a smaller way I have enacted something similar, probably around the same time that Atwood was writing her book. Coincidence? Who knows? For a long time I used to think that there was a dark, empty place located somewhere in the centre of myself. It bothered me, because I thought it was rather like Tarwater's familiar voice, a part of me that was innately bad and incurable. I figured that made sense, theologically, anyhow. In those years my friends and I used to do a lot of guided fantasy work, trying out for ourselves some Gestalt techniques we had learned. On a couple of occasions I imagined that I was walking through the woods, like Hansel and Gretel, and found a house with my name on the door. I went inside and saw a small, cosy place, just two rooms with a fireplace—something like the cottages that appear in some of the finer English detective stories, all beamed ceilings and chintz. I loved that fantasy house, enjoyed being in it. Some time later I told a friend, who knew about the black hole, that it had disappeared. I looked hard for it, thinking that perhaps it had shifted, was lurking somewhere, hiding behind a rib perhaps. But amazingly, it was gone.

I will probably never know, nor do I care, what that black hole really meant. Until this moment I have never connected it with my house fantasy, but now I wonder. Did the discovery of "my house" cause the black, empty space inside to go away? Did some sort of integration take place through the use of fantasy, as it did for Atwood's heroine, and in a different way for Tarwater? Today I live in a house with beamed ceilings, a fireplace and chintz. I live on a city street beside a large pleasant woods. I love the life I have here. Oh, Mr. Jung, what would you say to that?

8

— THE HOLY COMMUNITY —

The Lord says this:
I remember the affection of your youth,
the love of your bridal days:
you followed me through the wilderness,
through a land unsown.

Jeremiah 2:2

Either we all get to the Promised Land together as a people, or none of us does. Purely private good is an obsolete category.

Sandra Schneiders, *With Oil in Their Lamps: Faith, Feminism, and the Future*

After the rending comes the making whole.
If you think of a holy desert or wilderness community, perhaps the Cistercians, with their remote hideaways, come to mind. Or the third-century Desert Fathers, lurking in their Egyptian caves. Closer to our own lives is the Findhorn Community on the northeast coast of Scotland, where a core community has brought exuberant life to the bleak land and now trains visitors in spiritual as well as botanical skills. Still, they are different from us, because they have decided to take to the wilderness as their true home. This is not the biblical idea of the holy community.

Most of the later biblical writers, when they looked back on the old wilderness of the Exodus, did not find the Hebrew community holy at all. They described the people who were led there as bad, disobedient, recalcitrant losers. God gave them an unequalled opportunity for a full, rich life, and they blew it. They turned their backs on him and went the other way, bitching and whining all the time. God told them they would be punished, that none of the first-generation escapees from Egypt would make it out of the wilderness, and it was so. Thus, the prophets, looking back on this time, made the Hebrews into negative moral figures: see, people, look on your ancestors' behaviour and beware.

Their children did gain the land of promise, however. They must have listened and learned, if only because their lives depended on it. Perhaps this is the reason why, of all the later writers, only Jeremiah and Hosea see this period as a blessed time, a time when God and his people were having a honeymoon together. Although some people did not learn, were faithless, and wanted to turn back to slavery, the others endured the testing, accepted the commands, and were united as the special people of God. They became the holy community of the desert.

They are really rather like us. They are a mixed bag, some turned towards holiness and freedom, some aghast at the prospect. They are, none of them, wilderness dwellers like the monastic groups. They are there for a time to be exposed to the clear, unadulterated truth, to hear or not to hear, to advance or to go back. Theirs is a sojourn, not a home-steading—either a growing or a decaying.

We have seen a number of communal groups already, those that make their dwelling for a time in the wilderness. There is the temporary ill-fated community of explorers in *A Discovery of Strangers*, linked together with one goal but different interests. The ultimate need to survive brings out the best, and the worst, of their characters. Then there is the com-munity of the homeless in *King;* by its nature and because of the forces against it, it cannot hold together. What the people learn is another instance of the callousness of the urban dwellers around them, who rout them out of their bleak and crude domicile for profit. They are really a group of invisible scapegoats. *Endgame* is a communal group, certainly, but it is the last one on a devastated earth. For the characters in a play, there are no truthful voices to hear but their own, and these are probably lying. The story is a kind of inverted parody of Moses at the end of the road; in this play, there is no view of a good land ahead. Then there is the temporary community of young Jews hiding in the forest in *The Gates of the Forest*. The reality they come to grips with is horrid and fearful, but they must discover it and so move on. The only other choice is death. Perhaps they come closest in spirit to the biblical understanding of what the wilderness can do.

What makes the biblical wilderness community so distinctive is first that it has a purpose, which, while unclear (at least at the beginning) to the members, is deeply serious. Whatever they are going to discover matters very much to the rest of their lives. Next is the fact that the community has stripped away all but the necessities of living, and is even lacking some of those. (Not that the Hebrews, mostly slaves, had much to carry away with them, but at least there were roofs in Egypt.) The distractions of city life aren't there, either. Then there is the quality of impermanence: no one expects to stay in the wilderness forever, though many die there. I get the impression, though I don't know if it is a fair one, that the Hebrews were kept there for 40 years because it took that long for them to understand what God was telling them over and over, and he really didn't want to give up on them.

Compared to the severity of this long endurance test, my little sojourns into communal wilderness places seem frivolous, like taking a spiritual holiday at the beach with parasol, flippers, and sunscreen.

There have been canoe trips, a week long at most, with close or casual friends. By the end of the trip some friendships had deepened richly, because we had time to make them so. Hardships weren't severe, though: even if there were no other habitations in sight, we could usually find a campsite prepared by some other light adventurers. There have also been retreats with friends and strangers, a few days at a time, in forested settings, housed in plain, substantial lodgings. Wherever I've gone, looking for enrichment and quiet for my weakened spirit—such as at a monastery in the Pyrenees—there has always been a roof over my head, and a way of getting out when I needed to. That is not to say that I haven't had fresh insights in these places, and that my life hasn't been much better for them. I couldn't possibly say how; I just know that they have made a difference, even if bolts of lightning did not appear, nor guiding clouds, nor pillars of fire. Yet perhaps, as a friend of mine suggests, I am reluctant to take on the wilderness in its fullness, wanting to stay a holiday tripper all my days, firmly rooted in the city. The wilderness of deprivation, isolation, and determination of purpose may be only a fantasy of mine; when actually faced with it, I'd run away in terror. Yes, that's probably true.

If you are looking for a place to shut out the world, confront your peculiar self, and struggle with community building, there's nothing like an island. A little group of "castaways" on deserted Taransay, one of the Western Isles off the coast of Scotland, tried to do just that, using the tools and skills of their grandparents' era to survive for a year, all the while being filmed by a BBC TV crew that was staying in a mainland hotel. Islands aren't necessarily wildernesses, of course. Partly it depends on how big they are. It takes a piece of land as small as Iona, for instance, and as inhospitable, to draw a community to it and yet keep it out of harm's way, meaning, of course, away from the rest of us.

On an island you are face to face with yourself, and with your often-pathetic attempts at forming and sustaining a community. Without rules such as those St. Columba established for his monks on Iona, or those that the Iona Community has developed today, community building would be a touch-and-go affair. On the island to which you have come to stay for a time, you lose your previous social identity with its many functions and relationships. You are forced to devise a new identity in a place where everything is new, experience is less diluted, and there is possible danger to body and soul. Chances are, you will come away a different person than when you arrived.

On a BBC radio program, *Desert Island Discs*, that has been running for over half a century, listeners call in and ask to hear those works they would take with them if shipwrecked. I think there should be something similar for books. If I were stranded on a desert island one of the books I'd long for is A.L. Kennedy's *Everything You Need*, a novel about a group of people seeking enlightenment on a Welsh island.

I have fallen for this book, hook, line, and iridescent fish. I love the characters, their frozen fearfulness, their lascivious quirks and perks, their deep wounds and even deeper affection for each other spilled out in tentative, pathetic little bursts of tenderness, quickly withdrawn. I love the story, as it moves gradually, with little hiccups of ferocity and a few grisly touches, to show the importance of these odd persons to each other. I love the absurdity of it all: the insanity of the protracted search for the Ultimate Whatever; the screwball idea of collecting a group of neurotic, emotional cripples in one place and hoping to inspire them and have them inspire each other; the impossibility of any good coming of the relationship between a dysfunctional editor and his equally dysfunctional writer obsessed with the pain of a long-finished marriage. Most wonderful and central to it all is the hilariously unfolding saga of the novel's "hero" and his daughter.

Finally, what I love and giggle about and cheer is the author of all this, who can take us on a romp so delicious, so delicately tongue-in-cheek, and so utterly, movingly serious. I am like a child who sees *Snow White* for the first, or second, or ninth time, skipping from chuckles to apprehension to relief to tears, and back again in a twinkling. In my third reading I'm still doing it. It is indeed well titled, even if Kennedy didn't mean it that way.

This is a love story and a loving story. It tells the truth about the process of loving, whipping it round you like a wet sheet in the wind sometimes, at other times feathering your skin and your mind with a laughing grace. It is a fireside book to keep the snow out of sight and the wind from howling. It is a book for all seasons.

I do not want to tell the whole story. It should be a surprise the first time, and then the second time you can come back to it fondly, glee-fully. So, simply, here is the plot, here the community, and here the wilderness.

Nathan Staples belongs to a writer's community on Foal Island that is run by a former writer, Joe Christopher. When one of the members dies, leaving the community short of its mystical number of seven, Mary Lamb, a promising but as yet unpublished author, is invited to join for a seven-year apprenticeship. Her mentor will be Nathan, a famous writer of popular melodramatic fiction. She is the only one on the island who does not know that Nathan is her father.

This is, as I said, a love story: of a man, Nathan, for his wife, Maura, and his daughter, Mary. The tricky part is that neither woman knows it: Maura because she and Nathan have been separated for years, and Mary because her mother has told her that her father is dead. Nathan appears to Mary to be an oddly moody, secretive person who at one moment seems to hate her, at another to praise her. Nathan, afraid to hurt her, afraid to push her, afraid to tell her the truth, wanting to choose the right time, staggers clumsily around her, reeling with self-loathing and indecision, stupefied by his love and admiration for her. At the same time, he is still trapped in his devotion to Maura, which leads him to desperate, hopeless moves.

The island wilderness has a physical vagueness that seems appropriate, because in this novel the wilderness is overwhelmed by the community. There are sacred places, hidden refuges, a risky shoreline, and plenty of vegetation to screen the inhabitants from each other. We have no sense of direction here; we don't know how each person makes use of the island, whether by walking around its circumference, walking through the centre, or moving from one point to another. People go to visit each other in their separate dwellings, but they seldom catch sight of each other as they move about. A sense of the haphazardness of the place is perfectly in tune with the lives of the islanders.

In one strange way or another, almost everyone in the community has been powerfully affected by the natural environment, either on the island or elsewhere. Ruth, whom one of the other islanders compares to a mushroom, is obsessed with the time when she was bitten by a shark, and cannot stop talking about it. Lynda, looking for thrills beyond the island, decides to swim with the sharks, too, and returns to tell everyone. Louis, the ex-teacher and historian, is "one of Nature's welcomers," perhaps the person most at home on the island. He revels in the myths and stories that have been told about it. Joe, who loves the island most, nevertheless has his most precious experience in the desert:

> He was imagining the desert at evening and walking out and meeting its first kiss: the dissipating rush, the closing tenderness of mineral heat. He was remembering the scent of size, of a scale so monstrous it could strike him free of his personality, made him naked to his blood: the scent of time, or time's distillate—disinterested, arcane and horrifying. He'd loved it, had known he would love it, had been astonished only by the intensity of that love.

Only Richard, forgotten in his marriage to Lynda, seems to have no bearings, no connections with anything at all, until Lynda returns to him after her shark adventure.

Nathan and Mary are most truly linked to the island itself. Mary begins her writing in a cave she believes she inherited from a previous writer. The island grows on her, until she is restless when she is away from it. As she goes outside at night she listens to

> ...the encoded night: the nervous leaves and twig snaps, the starting of rabbits, the visible silence of owls and the reckless crash and snuffle of her local hedgehog rooting for a feed—the usual animal and vegetable hubbub, seasonally adjusted, and then amplified by the saturated dark. A fraction of moon spiked behind sails of hot

cloud, while half echoes caught in the wood fell stickily against her as she tried to understand why they all seemed different tonight.

Her fondness for Nathan and her connectedness to the island grow together. Nathan's great joy is to show Mary the secret spiral pattern in a hollow on the Head, the island's high point:

Then the climb took over and they panted their way to the sudden clarity of the summit, a slightly rounded oval, hunched under the moving air, risen out of the sea's horizontal imagination. Mary wanted to sit for a while in the wiry grass, but Nathan shooed her on. "You can rest in a minute, it's just a bit further—go on." He loved this part: the gentle ascent across the softly domed surface here always made him think of walking over a tiny planet, his own space. "Now. Then. What do you think of that?"

As he and Mary grow closer, his moods become so cheerful that not even the unexpected fall of snow can dismay him. In fact, he loves it, just as Eckless, his dog, does:

The first emotion he met on waking was no longer dismay. And he couldn't deny that, like Eckless, he'd been lifted by the happy accident of snow. Its icicle jab at his lung was invigorating and he'd already spent at least an hour this morning mesmerized by the padded descent of another shower. And as for the smoothing of the island to one big ripple of blameless white—that could only seduce every Calvinist muscle in his soul.

There are two other geographical points in this novel where Nathan and Mary go on occasion, always returning to the island. One is the village where Mary has been gently raised by her "uncles," her mother's gay brother and his companion. On the island, faced with Nathan's abruptness and uncanny ability to put his foot in his mouth, Mary is homesick at first for their kindly ways. Gradually, though, she misses them less and the island becomes her real home. The other is Nathan's off-island home, London, where he goes to visit his friend and editor Jack Grace, and where he keeps an unlovely apartment. Publishing parties, too much alcohol, and Jack's self-destruction make his visits to London a disaster. The island is really his only home; in contrast to the city it is balm and rescue for the heart.

The wilderness exists for a purpose: to allow the islanders to retreat from ordinary life to write words of power, share insights, and experience the ultimate. Joe encourages them to take life-threatening risks, to teeter at the brink of death, in order to achieve this. "Joe's personal theory was that Technicolor, widescreen contact with the Beyond would infallibly compose itself into clear, metaphysical sense." They will not merely be like those people who, inspired by Emerson, took to the woods and returned, says Belden C. Lane, "full of nothing but themselves, their pockets stuffed with metaphors."[27] These islanders will write from the core of their new beings.

In the end, the wilderness is sandblasted by the writing itself. No matter how you twist and turn this novel, gleefully and satisfyingly unfolding the story lines, embracing the groups of people each by each, it stands out as a book about writing, about the way of words and the why of language. It is not only about the power of words; it shows that power on every page, in every conceivable mood and tone and rhythm.

It is Louis, the keen historian, who first tells why writing matters:

Death and language—each is the opposite and complement of the other. What do you think, hm? If you aren't going to die, why bother writing? Why else put all that effort into something that stays behind. How do you understand you're already dying and that others are already dead? Because there is already writing. Extinction and explanation, the theft and the gift.

Nathan, as Mary's mentor, makes the case for telling the truth, not disguising it behind devious or duplicitous language.

I don't want to be *informed*, I want to be *educated*, and I don't want to be *enabled*, I want to be *helped*, and I don't want something *new*, I want something *better*, and I don't want to be *offered choices*, I want to be *free*. I have spent a great deal of my life learning to love what words *mean*. Especially the bad ones, the ones that need careful watching. Assassination, removal, termination, problem-solving, taking out, euthanasia, cleansing, special handling, natural wastage, merciful release, killing, murder—I do understand that these are all very much the same thing. Offer me an euphemism, a circumlocution, a truth economy…and I will be moved to pulp your brain, to lop off your hands, to draw out your…tongue with pincers and roast it before your eyes—because you are not using what you've been given properly.

Here is his estimation of Richard, who Mary says looks "very dashing" with one arm smaller than the other:

And that would clinch it obviously—dashing deformity—must be a writer. The fact that he can only cough up genre crime yarns and post-modernist ragbags of Alzheimered tat should not be taken into consideration.

At the conclusion of his attack on language abuse, Nathan shows Mary how much words matter to him, caressing them in speech:

Sometimes, at the heart of me, there won't fall a word, there will be nothing but the wait. But then it comes, it speaks, it's there for me and I am there for it. We give ourselves to each other, we each possess the other, we agree. And after that, nothing can stop us. Not even me.

At the same time that Nathan is teaching his very capable student/daughter about the power of language, Kennedy shows the two of them floundering about in their attempts to please one another, being misunderstood, becoming furious or ashamed, and walking off in a huff. Nathan's behaviour is incomprehensible to Mary; his words seem harsh and uncaring, and all the while he is trying his best not to disturb her. Much of the lightly ironic humour comes from our knowledge of the outrageous thoughts that hover around the completely ordinary dialogue of the main characters. The conversation that starts them on the road to true expression of their love for each other is a kind of truce over the use of the word "nice," a word that Nathan deplores. At one point they don't speak for a year, owing to one of these verbal misunderstandings.

"You said it was nice to see me."
Anxiety lapped between his shoulder blades. "Yes? Um. Did I?"
"You did."
He couldn't think where this was going, almost didn't want to know.
"You don't like *nice*. You think it's a bad word."
"There are no bad words." He risked a look at her—got no clues.
"And I'm never all that eloquent when I'm semi-unconscious." But

there was a growing softness about her mouth, he could see
that.... "It was—I'm sorry—very nice."
"You're sorry it was nice?"
"No, I'm not sorry...."
She was smirking. Cheeky...lovely wee woman: she was
cuddling Ruth and also laughing at him. In a *nice* way, laughing.
"No, I'm *not* sorry. I'm not sorry at all."

It is Joe who compares the process of writing with going out into
the desert. He tells Mary,

> "In the desert you'll never quite know what things are, not at first.
> The absence of scale and the presence of heat will tend to mislead
> you: one man standing might just as easily be a rock, a truck, a
> camel, a tent: you can't tell. Unfamiliar elements will beguile you,
> but your best course is still to proceed. You'll only know if you go.
> And see. Then everything will show you itself, will tell you its na-
> ture, when you're close enough."

> "This is a metaphor, right?"

> "If you'd like, Mary Lamb, if you'd like. Or a small token of my
> esteem on the occasion of your making your start with words. A
> clean, indoor job—you might like it—writing."

Joe has done us the double favour of showing why one should enter
the wilderness, or at least what is possible there, and of giving the answer to the question that underlies all of this book: Why bother to write
about the wilderness? Why read about it, in fact? My answer in this
moment is to point to this book, to say, because the wilderness we see
here is a gift, a reminder. It shows that the world is not entirely cluttered
with the ordinary appurtenances of living, or with the fruitless palaver
of talking heads, or with the busy work of going from crowded room to
crowded room. It is a reminder so necessary that without it we'd easily
dismiss the possibility of finding open lyrical spaces where one might
freely wander, of random landscapes in which to refit cracked and en-
crusted minds. It is one of the great repositories of *mana*, that divine
power that can change human lives by showing itself in one way or
another. Writing is about making a case for living, and writing about the
wilderness is one way of pointing out, perhaps tapping into, that *mana*.

If you cannot conceive of voyaging into a deserted place, think of the island, or the wilderness, as a time in your life, not a space, and the mainland or city as another time. Then reading a book like this is like being on an island, a reflective place, from which the everyday is for the most part excluded. Reading is a time to discover your own wilderness and what it is saying to you. Don't tell me reading is not as good as being there. In reading you enter into the "there" of the book, and it all depends—on me, on the literature I am reading, on the circumstances in which I read—how significant being there is. My vision of the wilderness comes as much, perhaps more, through reading than through beating the bushes. But that's me. Let's just say that the experiences are different, and that there are many ways through the desert that take you to the promised land.

Not every truth-seeking community succeeds in a modest or superlative way. Just because you set out with high hopes doesn't mean that those hopes are either realistic or suitably directed. You could fail miserably, be reduced to bleating and grovelling in the desert, left with only one alternative to a failed and dismal life.

Eugene Ionesco's *Les Chaises* (*The Chairs*) shows how it's done. In this play one can see what happens when a sojourn in the wilderness is sustained by looking backwards and by having false hopes for the future. The effect of such nostalgia for the past (a past that is not truly remembered, at that), and of fantasizing an improbable future, is to turn the noble ideas we associate with the biblical wilderness—of community, of leadership, of proclamation, and of the divine message—into parodies of the originals. *Les Chaises*, in expressing the hunger for a lost Eden of childhood, shows the failure of post-Edenic wilderness people to achieve the promised land. Bad faith on the part of human beings is matched by bad faith on the part of God.

Two nonagenarians, presumably husband and wife, live by themselves on an island in a house that is bare of everything except two chairs. The setting immediately reminds one of *Endgame*, but watch out for the important differences in tone, in the behaviour of the people towards each other, in their expectations for their lives and for the world. We discover gradually that the Old Man is the concierge of the house, and that, at the end of their lives, he has summoned up enough courage to deliver his crucial message to the world that he is confident will receive it gratefully. The content of that message, however, is never given, nor does the Old Man intend to deliver it himself: he is too nervous for that and has hired an orator to speak for him.

Guests who have been invited to hear the message begin to arrive at the island, but they are all invisible. The Old Man and the Old Woman run back and forth finding chairs for them all, until the room is filled with these invisible guests. The couple hold one-sided conversations, pausing for the inaudible responses. Finally, the last guest, the Emperor, arrives, and soon after, the Orator. Having welcomed his audience and expressed his gratitude to everyone who has made this event possible, the Old Man and the Old Woman commit suicide, jumping from separate windows into the water.

The Orator commences speaking, but he is a deaf-mute and can only mumble incomprehensibly. Growing angry because he is not being understood, he writes letters on a board, but the only ones that spell any known word are ANGEPAIN ("angelbread") and ADIEU. He stalks off haughtily, and laughter is heard from the invisible audience.

The wilderness in this play is a waste place—a house that the two occupants do not own, empty of furniture except for two chairs and a gas lamp, on an island from which boats may be seen at a great distance. Nothing enters in, and the two old people do not go out. (Some members of the family did visit them ten years ago, the Old Woman says, but even this may be her fantasy. As we will see, neither of their memories are to be trusted.) The wireless, the telephone, and the daily newspapers are mentioned but never seen, and it is likely that they do not exist. The Old Man tells the Old Woman to drink her tea: the staging comment is, "Naturally, there is no tea." As the old couple brings in more and more (real) chairs for the guests, the room becomes so crowded that the two are unable to get through to reach each other. These chairs, brought in through the various stage doors in a random way, do not belong to them but to the owner of the house. The effect of a roomful of chairs, occupied by invisible people with whom the couple converse, is to make the place seem even more desolate than it was at the beginning of the play. This barrenness is very different from that of the biblical image of stripping away one's possessions in order to be open to the desert vision and instruction.

The isolation and the sense of waste are made more forceful by the noted absence of certain people. Their son has left at the age of seven, finding his parents too cruel, says the Old Woman. The Old Man says that they never had any children. The Old Man mourns the fact that he is an orphan, and refuses to be comforted by the Old Woman when she offers to be his mother. Wistful memories of a garden with wet grass that they were unable to enter, and of a city of light, are a contrast to the island with its solitary house. It seems that the Old Man is the caretaker of nothing worth caring for.

Because of the characters' names, their ages of 94 and 95, their memory of a garden to which they were refused re-entry, and the nature of their present habitat, it is an easy surmise that these are Adam and Eve 80 years after their expulsion from Eden. At one point, the Old Woman says, "For me, the branch of the apple-tree is broken." The city they remember, she thinks, is called Paris. She says, "Paris? There never was such a place, my pet," and the Old Man says, "There must have been once, because it fell into ruins." Paris may be a false memory of "Paradise."

In another allusion, though, the Old Woman is called Semiramis by her husband. He is referring either to the Babylonian queen who built the wondrous hanging gardens or to the Assyrian queen who built Nineveh with its 15 gates (the set has 10 stage doors). This is another of his false memories, brought in to shore up his ruins. The Old Woman is certainly no queen, nor he a king.

Waste, absence, isolation underline the vacuity of two wasted lives, obsessed with the past, living off false memories and unrealistic hopes for the future. They are not even has-beens, but, in their view, might-have-beens. "You might have become a President General, a General Director, or even a General Physician or a Postmaster-General, if you'd wanted to, if you'd had just a little ambition in life," says the Old Woman. As it is, the Old Man is "Quartermaster-General"—a caretaker—but the Old Woman insists on referring to him as "General." Each evening for the last 75 years the Old Woman has asked to hear the story of their arrival at the garden gate, and their being turned away. While this episode may have been a true part of their past, its repetition as story hints that they have done nothing much else in the intervening years.

The Old Man lives for the most part in his childish past, sitting on his wife's knee, receiving her comfort as he moans that he is an orphan, and recalling the moment when, on his father's lap, he had his one chance to deliver his message of hope for the world.

One day, after the evening meal, I was sitting on my father's lap, as usual, before I went to bed...my moustache was bigger than his, and more pointed...my chest more hairy...my hair already turning grey, his was still brown...we had some visitors, grown-up people, at table and they started laughing, laughing....

And then I thought: But I'm not married yet. So I must still be a child.

His other important memory, of his mother's death, haunts him, but whether with guilt or only with his own suffering is not made plain. He left her in a ditch beseeching him not to go while he went to a dance. When he came back she was dead, her grave undiscoverable. He is the one who has suffered, "but not the others."

The antidote for this suffering and the longing for his mother is to deliver his message at last, and for this reason the guests are invited to the island. The non-appearance of the guests introduces the greatest sense of unreality to the play. With the two different versions of their past that the old couple tell, the question of the play's reality is left unsettled. In conversing with the guests, for instance, the husband says that they have had no children, while the wife describes their son's leaving home. The husband tells the story of abandoning his mother, but the wife says that he was always very kind to his parents and that they died in his arms. The impression derived from the "presence" of the invisible guests and from the differing views of the past is that reality for these two is subjective. Sometimes they come up with an agreed-upon view of the past, but even that may be untrue, although we'll never know what "true" is. That a caretaker should have either the status or the knowledge to draw the Emperor to his empty island house to hear his world-shaking message is obviously preposterous.

The final action of the play produces irony, but the basis for the irony is uncertain, too. In full confidence that the Orator will finally give the world the message that will "dazzle posterity with the enlightenment I bring," man and wife jump to their deaths. The Orator, in turn, bows to the audience and leaves. Sounds of laughter gradually fade away, and the play ends with the departure of both audiences, real and invisible.

There are several possible ways to look at this ending. The first is that since the reality within which the old people live is both subjective and ignoble, no message from them could be either true or worthwhile. Their hopes for the future are just as misdirected as their remembrance of the past. Second, one might say that all three visible characters, who agree that a message coming from a source outside oneself can benefit humankind, are wrong.

The third possibility, if you look at the Adam and Eve parallels, is to say that in the world that is built following the expulsion, God is also deaf and dumb, just as his people are hollow, cruel, and obsessively nostalgic. The situation in Eden is over: what God could say in the garden he is no longer able to say. In the Old Man's introduction of the Orator, he thanks everyone who has made the evening possible: "The owners of this building, the architect, and the masons who were kind enough to raise these walls!... All those who dug the foundations...." A long list of sponsors follows, ending with, "Thanks once more, and above all, to our well-loved Sovereign, His Majesty the Emperor...." This is an ironic exchange for God's creative action.

A final interpretation would combine all three thoughts in this way: since subjective reality is all there is to go on in this play, one must say that the Orator has delivered the appropriate message—that is, no message. Taking it as the play's statement that people do live in these subjective circles of reality, separate from each other's, no message from outside can be given that they can understand. (In fact, they don't even try; they commit suicide.) From this wilderness there is no way out, through either internal or external means. Human beings continue to live in a false past, an unreal present and a foolish expectation for the future. No divine vision will alter this. The wilderness is a no-possibility place.

So the biblical wilderness into which one goes to become a united community, prepared to enter the Promised Land, has become a parody in *Les Chaises*. There is no true community; even the family is a distorted one, and ironically the old couple cannot even die together, separated as they are by the crowd. The relationship between God and his people has been severed by fault on both sides. To remain in the wilderness is death, but there is no other place to go.

Just as the holy community of the desert, as the prophets term it, is composed of all sorts of people joined together by one vision and one directive, so is Kennedy's writers' community. In a parodic inversion, Ionesco's island group also resembles the biblical image. Where they all differ is in the outcome of the narrative. We know that some, but not all, of the Hebrews reached the Promised Land. We sense, by the open-endedness of *Everything You Need*, that Mary and perhaps Nathan are on their way. We have no such conviction about the characters in *The Chairs*. For Ionesco in this play, the world is the wilderness, inescapable and inevitable.

9

— A VOICE IN THE WILDERNESS —

You ask, what can she do for you? Many things. First she is unavoidable. Test it, and you will find she is unavoidable. And this is what you need, as you are an avoider.... She will make consciousness to shine. She will burnish you. She will force the present moment upon you.

Saul Bellow, *Henderson the Rain King*

When the Lord will come to the soul, and draw it into communion with himself, he will have his way hereto prepared in the Desert; not in the throng of a City, but in a solitary Desert place, he will allure us, and draw us into the wilderness, from the company of men, when he will speak to our heart, and when he prepares our heart to speak unto him.

Peter Bulkeley, *Gospel-Covenant; or, the Covenant of Grace Opened* (1651)

There are some mysterious caverns in this world that I hope we will never fathom, or if they are exposed to light, that I will not find out about it. I don't want to know, for instance, whether animals dream when they hibernate, or if fish can hear us, Dylan Thomas' child's question. I don't want to find out some day that through instrumentation the very last and lowest Trojan city has been discovered, or absolutely all the burial sites of the Irish kings, or the original habitat of the Romany. I want people to keep on trying to find out these things, but hope that the pursuit is endless. That way we can still imagine.

Which brings me to the greatest mystery of them all: the human mind. For all that ordinary folk like me know, after we have learned that certain parts of the brain have specific functions, we still do not know how it all works together, or how it takes up with the rest of our being to traffic with the world. I don't know what causes me to imagine, or even to want to imagine. I don't know why I think sometimes in crooked lines and patches of colour, sometimes linearly. Sometimes I think I feel my way into discoveries, sometimes I intuit. Seldom is it by logic alone that I come to know things. I may sound rational, even now, but that isn't how I get to the place where I am.

Many people will say that this kind of knowing, be it circular, or sideways, or like a blast from the ether or the gut, is the most important kind there is. It reveals what we most desire to know. When we try to express it, and to say how it came about, the only way we can describe it is metaphorically, in images.

Some saints arrive at this most profound, most intimate knowing through visions. The prophets learn through listening, and the image they use is the voice of God. Hearing this voice is enough to change their lives and the direction of sacred history.

The most vivid description of an encounter with the voice of God is Elijah's—he must have told it to someone, for he was alone at the time. Having walked for 40 days and 40 nights in the wilderness to escape the wrath of Jezebel, he reaches Mount Horeb, where he rests in a cave. God tells him to go outside and he will come.

> Then [the LORD] himself went by. There came a mighty wind, so strong it tore the mountains and shattered the rocks before [the LORD]. But [the LORD] was not in the wind. After the wind came an earthquake. But [the LORD] was not in the earthquake. After the earthquake came a fire. But [the LORD] was not in the fire. And after the fire there came the sound of a gentle breeze....Then a voice came to him, which said, "What are you doing here, Elijah?"

The Lord orders Elijah to return and anoint two kings, who will wage war against Ahab and his vengeful wife, and to anoint Elisha as his successor.

Once again, the wilderness is the locale for this momentous event, as it is for Jesus, for Moses, and in a different way for John the Baptist. We don't know what John was doing there or how long he stayed; what we do know, says Matthew, is that "he preached in the wilderness of Judea and this was his message: 'Repent, for the kingdom of heaven is close at hand.'" That insight was the most powerful one he ever had, and it certainly changed his life.

Insight, visions, voices can come when and where you least expect them, in wildernesses, and especially on mountains, although don't rule out the desert plains, the forests, the valleys. In *La montagne secrète*, Pierre has his vision of the numinous, the beyond, by simply seeing the mountain, not climbing to its summit. In the forest, Gregor meets the mysterious Gavriel (is he another emanation from God, an embodied voice?), the memory of whom sustains him through his ordeals. In the wilderness of *Surfacing* the heroine's vision takes place underwater, a nice metaphorical way to undergo rebirth, or baptism.

All these people are seeking something of great value that would give their lives some relief from traumas, some context of contentment. Whether they choose the wilderness or are forced into it, it becomes for them a place of temporary refuge and permanent renewal. They aren't strangers to the wilderness, though; they know something of its power already.

My next two contemporary heroes are a little boy who knows the wilderness well, and a great hulking misfit of a man who knows only that he must go there in order to save himself. I'll begin with the latter, because there seems to be a symbiosis between Nathan Staples in Wales and Eugene Henderson of Boston, the hero of Saul Bellow's *Henderson the Rain King*. Henderson was one of my first loves, Nathan a recent one, and I am beginning to wonder what attracts me to these wacko, emotional shipwrecks who are intelligent enough to know what they are, and distraught enough to foul up every attempt at self-recovery. I suppose in the end it's because the authors of these novels have so much fun with their heroes, and it's catching.

Henderson violates all my stereotypes. With a huge frame, a whacking great nose, a trumpet-shaped voice, and the uncanny ability to sound the wrong notes wherever he goes, he's not my idea of old-moneyed, ex-Ivy League New England. Yet he's one of the best examples I know of twentieth-century dilemmas on the hoof. His blunders are crafty, deliberate—not uncontrolled actions at all—but we don't have any idea why he makes them. He sets himself up, but for fun or misery we cannot tell. If he has plotted schemes he wishes to carry out against people, we never know why or to what end. At least when Petruchio gives Kate a merry hard time in *The Taming of the Shrew*, we know he's trying to tame her. What Henderson has in mind towards his wife Lily is his alone to know. He's confessional, foolishly antagonistic, and even more foolishly kind, like someone whose wires are running off in all directions. Like the cables connected to my computer, all twisted over and under each other and likely to give trouble because I haven't turned the termination switch to on—or is it off?—Henderson, too, hasn't found the switch.

The plot: it's a quest story, in which our hero leaves home to seek his version of the Grail and has adventures along the way (misadventures, too) from which he manages to extricate himself and escape. Whether he actually achieves his Grail the reader must decide, as Bellow doesn't give the answer. Henderson is a Gawain type, rash, intemperate, given to acting before thinking about the consequences, or not giving a damn about them. Propelled by a desperate voice within him saying, "I want, I want," Henderson decides to leave his family and buys a one-way ticket to Africa. Led by an African guide, Romilayu, he travels deeper and darker until he comes to a lovable tribe called the Arnewi. From the queen he receives affection and insight, from her sister a proposal of marriage, so to speak. But everything changes when Henderson decides to rid the tribe's well of frogs, so that their precious cattle may drink, and by mistake destroys the well itself. Mortified, he and Romilayu leave, the sounds of the tribe's wailing in their ears.

Moving on through the wilderness, meeting no one, they finally arrive at the home of the Wariri, whose king, Dahfu, has been greatly praised by his friend Itelo of the Arnewi. Henderson hopes that Dahfu has not heard of the disaster he has caused the Arnewi, but if he has, it doesn't seem to matter to the king, who is delighted with his new friend. The plot gets complicated here, as it leads up to the acclamation of Henderson as Sungo, the Rain King, who has brought rain to the land.

Henderson confesses to Dahfu his need for some kind of salvation, something of which Dahfu is already quite aware, and for which he has the remedy. Although a brave man physically, Henderson is, as Dahfu says, an avoider, and must learn to confront his fears. This can be done by spending time in the presence of Dahfu's pet (more like his friend), a lion that he keeps in the basement of the palace. Henderson, Dahfu, and Atti the lioness spend every morning together, until the king receives word that another lion he is seeking has been discovered. This lion, supposedly the soul of his dead father, must be captured before Dahfu can be properly deemed to be king. In the course of the lion hunt, Dahfu is killed, and Henderson, who is fingered to be the next king, escapes. He goes back to the States bearing the lion cub, which is believed to be his friend Dahfu.

Of course, the plot is mad, the events hilarious (I won't tell you more), made even funnier by Henderson's assumptions and behaviour among these people he does not understand. He pours out his true confessions, his view of the universe, his observations of what is going on around him to people who know very little English, and whose reply is often "Oh no, suh." His responses to the strangeness he encounters are sensible to him but have an altogether different meaning to the Africans. When he is put in a hut to spend his first night with the Wariri and finds a corpse there, his reaction is, they're trying to frame me with his murder, and so he carries the body to the ravine and dumps it. The true reason for the body in the hut comes out only at the end of the story, and it is in part a ritualistic one, and also a test of Henderson's strength.

Henderson the Rain King is a picture book, a sensuous book, full of images that sound, of bodies with pains reeling off the page, of skies that sing, people that tingle with oil and heat, singing and dancing and shouting and weeping. This book is curvaceous, not flat, full of pulsing sentiment, not detachedly chill. Henderson is the cause of it all, and we inhale the world through him, touch, smell, and sound. He sees in strong colour, always mixed with other sensations. Here he is in the empty desert "all simplified and splendid":

> The mountains were naked, and often snakelike in their forms, without trees, and you could see the clouds being born on the slopes. From this rock came vapor, but it was not like ordinary vapor, it cast a brilliant shadow.... At night, after Romilayu had prayed, and we lay on the ground, the face of the air breathed back on us, breath for breath. And then there were the calm stars, turning around and singing, and the birds of the night with heavy bodies, fanning by.... When I laid my ear to the ground I thought I could hear hoofs. It was like lying on the skin of a drum.

His emotions ripple and roar through every part of his body as he experiences the world as beautiful or fearful or strange. His landscapes become truly inscapes, indwellings. On the morning of the day he prepares to give a great boon to the Arnewi by restoring their water supply, he wakes up excited and goes outside.

...what happened was like nothing previously conceived; it took the form merely of the light at daybreak against the white clay of the wall beside me and had an extraordinary effect, for right away I begin to feel the sensation in my gums warning of something lovely, and with it a close or painful feeling in the chest.... I had to put down the baked yam I was chewing and support myself with my hands on the ground, for I felt the world sway under me and I would have reached, if I were on a horse, for the horn of the saddle.

There is plenty that is biblical about Henderson; in fact, he could be a prophet in modern dress (stained jockey shorts, T-shirt, white sun helmet, and crepe soles), self-deprecations and all. When he is not forced into fasting in the desert, his diet seems to be mainly yams. He attempts minor miracles of fire (igniting a bush with his lighter) and water (bombing the well), and the major one of bringing rain, although he doesn't believe he is really the agent of that one. Although he seems like an Elijah or a John the Baptist—he proposes to go out to the desert and eat locusts—the prophetic role is reversed when he meets Dahfu, who is the one to guide him towards the truth he seeks.

Henderson is not at odds with the world; of reality he says, "I love the old bitch just the way she is." It is himself that he is at odds with. He believes that truth comes in blows, and so it seems to happen for him, with the frogs' disaster, the lioness, the king's death. He thinks that his spirit is asleep, and that suffering is the only way to burst that sleep. Then he asks, "How shall a man be broken for whom reality has no fixed dwelling!" This is the confusion not of a philosopher, but of a seething crater, mad with fever. During the rain ceremony, he thinks,

> "I was excited to the bursting point. I swelled, I was sick, and my blood circulated peculiarly through my body—it was turbid and ecstatic both. It prickled within my face, especially in the nose, as if it might begin to discharge itself there. And as though a crown of gas were burning from my head, so I was tormented."

"Oh, my body, my body!" he cries. "Why have we never really got together as friends?" A man who describes himself as a "giant turnip" or a "giant collection of errors" is no one's mentor. He needs help, and he knows it. It's just a question of where to find it.

Some of the help comes from within. The voice that cries "I want, I want" has brought him to the remoteness of Africa, and it is his own character and sensitivity that persuade others with the power to help him. He recognizes that power, too, first in the two women of the Arnewi, the queen Willatale and her sister Mtalba. When he meets the queen, she places his hand between her breasts, the usual manner of greeting.

> On top of everything else, I mean the radiant heat and the monu-
> mental weight which my hand received, there was the calm pulsa-
> tion of her heart participating in the introduction. This was as regular
> as the rotation of the earth, and it was a surprise to me; my mouth
> came open and my eyes grew fixed as if I were touching the secrets
> of life....

Willatale tells him that he wants to live, *grun-tu-molani*. Henderson is ecstatic that she knows this. "Not only I molani for myself, but for everybody. I could not bear how sad things have become in the world and so I set out because of this molani. Grun-tu-molani, old lady—old queen. Grun-tu-molani, everybody."

It is the day after this revelation that Henderson has his daybreak vision, which appears equally as a voice. "Throughout my life," he thinks, "I had known these moments when the dumb begins to speak, when I hear the voices of objects and colors; then the physical universe starts to wrinkle and change and heave and rise and smooth, so it seems that even the dogs have to lean against a tree, shivering."

The most important voice is that of the king, Dahfu, who was in his third year of medical school when he was called home by the death of his father. He knows that his lifeline is determined by his virility, and that when he is no longer capable, he will be strangled. (In real life, this is or was the fate of the head of the Shilluk tribe of the upper-Nilotic Sudan.) Yet he returns to carry out his duties as king. On their first meeting Henderson says, "...there was something about this man that gave me the conviction that we could approach ultimates together." He knows the king can change him. "The king's eyes gleamed into mine with such a power of significance that I felt he could, if he wanted to, pass right straight into my soul. He could invest it." Henderson sees Dahfu as a Be-er, himself as a Becomer. "I've just got to stop Becoming. Jesus Christ, when am I going to Be? I have waited a hell of a long time."

Dahfu's course of training to turn Henderson into a Be-er is to introduce him to Atti the lioness, to bring him into her den and allow Atti to
familiarize herself with him, so that he and Dahfu can begin the real
work. Dahfu instructs Henderson to observe Atti carefully, and then
imitate her. She is a Be-er.

> But first by means of the lion try to distinguish the states that are
> given and the states that are made. Observe that Atti is all lion.
> Does not take issue with the inherent. Is one hundred percent within
> the given.

Henderson begins his lessons.

> And so I was the beast. I gave myself to it, and all my sorrow came
> out in the roaring. My lungs supplied the air but the note came
> from my soul. The roaring scalded my throat and hurt the corners
> of my mouth and presently I filled the den like a bass organ pipe.
> This was where my heart had sent me, with its clamor.

Eventually something begins to change. "The roaring I had done, I
believe, had loosened my whole structure and liberated some things
that belonged at the bottom." He has begun to do what Dahfu wishes,
to break the cycle of fear and desire. He tells Romilayu at the end of the
story that he has broken the spirit's sleep. He does not understand the
ways of the universe, and the bad days of his suffering keep returning to
plague him. Still, he says, "I believe there is justice, and that much is
promised."

The last we see of Henderson, on his way home to Lily and the kids,
he is running round and round the plane, which has stopped down on
the Newfoundland ice, holding an orphaned Persian child in his arms.
Will he enter medical school as he says he will? Of course we don't
know, but given his character, which is becoming enlightened but still
remains intransigently out of line, I doubt it. In other words, the novel
does not promise happily-ever-after salvation to those who listen to their
inner and outer voices. What the voice tells you is only the beginning.

There are revelations and revelations. To Henderson, who builds
his life into melodrama at all costs, revelation comes like a blow, as a
terrible confrontation with the force of being, with a devastating death.
He wouldn't hear the still, small voice of reality all around him: he's too
occupied with lifting gigantic stone figures and listening to the groans

of his own insides. In complete contrast is the hero of W.O. Mitchell's *Who Has Seen the Wind*, Brian O'Connal, to whom revelations come in small, quiet ways as befits his age and size.

When the novel begins, Brian is four years old. The book is chiefly his story, as he grows up in a prairie town in Saskatchewan, and discovers the extremities of life experiences—birth, pain, suffering, cruelty, hatred, dying and death. At the same time, Mitchell traces the characters and encounters of the people whose lives intersect directly or obliquely with Brian's—a colourful group, ranging from righteous religious bigots, to hypocritical wafflers, to the outcasts and wildly outrageous who are closest in heart and mind to the core symbol of this novel, the wilderness as wind-swept prairie.

In the short period of Brian's life shown in the novel, between the ages of four and 12, he suffers two nasty incidents with his teacher in his first year of school, he watches his dog being trampled to death by a horse, and he loses his father and later his grandmother, the two people who were closest to him. Many other minor events show him the world as it is for everyone, a mixed blessing. Brian looks and listens with all his heart, as he tries to make sense of it all. On the prairie, he finds both questions and illumination.

The biblical wilderness is typically unsown land, used for grazing, for forest, or for nothing at all. The prairie here is of course sown with wheat, but because of the years of drought it is burnt and dry. What crops there are are patchy and thin. This is the way the adults see the prairie, for the most part. What Brian and a few others see is its vastness, its wildness, its freedom from human control. The wind blows when and how it chooses, doing what it wills to the crops. During these drought years it brings black dust out of the parched earth and causes cracks and spoiled crops. The wind makes the prairie either wasted or wild. To Brian its wild beauty is predominant: here he experiences both delight and anguish in relation to all that is libertine—the weeds and flowers, the meadow larks, the gophers. The prairie impresses him with its otherness:

> Prairie's awful, thought Brian, and in his mind there loomed vaguely fearful images of a still and brooding spirit, a quiescent power unsmiling from everlasting to everlasting to which the coming and passing of the prairie's creatures was but incidental.

He recognizes the horrors for prairie beings of captivity—an owl kept in a cage and of thoughtless cruelty—another boy swinging the tail off a gopher. He sees in the Young Ben, who lives on the prairie with his alcoholic father, the spirit of the prairie. The prairie belongs to Ben, and Ben belongs to no one, and to no social or religious morality.

Above all the prairie has a voice, and its chief voice is the wind. "All around him," Brian feels, "the wind was in the grass with a million timeless whisperings. A forever-and-forever sound it had, forever and for never." Brian has been attentive to this voice ever since he first explored the prairie at the age of four. He hears the sounds of crickets, grasshoppers, telephone lines, and gophers, but above all, he hears the wind, "and all about him...a pervasive sighing through great emptiness, unhampered by the buildings of the town, warm and living against his face and in his hair."

It is the voice of the wind in the wilderness that causes Brian to ask most of his questions, about life's value and its direction—the same question answered by the book's epigraph: "As for man, his days are as grass: as a flower of the field, so he flourisheth. For the wind passeth over it, and it is gone; and the place thereof shall know it no more." The wind and the land over which it blows are eternal and implacable; with the death of his father, Brian comes to grips with the understanding that people come and go, endlessly.

What is beautiful and what is ugly about the prairie—the dead gopher, for example—are set in the context of meaning and mystery. The meaning of the prairie cannot be verbalized but remains as symbol, translucent, not transparent. As such it evokes what Brian calls "the feeling," powerful yet unspecific. It comes to him first at age six, as a sense of elation "of such fleeting delicacy and poignancy that he dared not turn his mind to it for fear that he might spoil it, that it might be carried away as lightly as one strand of spider web on a sigh of a wind." He finds it next in small things, sights, sounds, and smells. "A tiny garden toad became suddenly magic for him one summer day—the smell of leaf mold, and clover, and wolf willow. Always, he noted, the feeling was most exquisite upon the prairie or when the wind blew." With the sight of a dead two-headed calf, the feeling changes. "It possessed an uncertain and breathless quality; he felt as though he were on a tightrope high in the air....Brian felt that he was staring at something he should not be staring at." Brian is beginning to know what Rudolf Otto describes as the awe and sense of otherness that belong to the experience of the holy, combined with the attractiveness of the earlier experiences. Listening to the old eccentric, Saint Sammy, hurl his imprecations against the village into the air, the feeling returns, and with it the longing to capture it and understand it: "That was all he wanted—one look. More than anything!"

The feeling disappears for a long time. When it does return, it is associated with the death of his beloved grandmother. He wonders about death, and about why one lives. He knows the direction in which to look:

> It had something to do with dying; it had something to do with being born. Loving something and being hungry were with it too. He knew that much now. There was the prairie; there was a meadow lark, a baby pigeon, and a calf with two heads. In some haunting way the Ben was part of it. So was Mr. Digby...
>
> ...
>
> Some day. The thing could not hide from him forever.

In this novel the wilderness is paramount. Mitchell has described his setting as a prairie encircling a town, not as a town set on a prairie. The inhabitants of the town are either indifferent to the prairie, hostile to it, an active part of it, or, like Brian, deeply moved by it. Their attitude to the prairie is reflected in their behaviour towards other people and towards the land. Among the anti-wilderness types are the religiously and socially pretentious, the ringleaders being the Reverend Mr. Powelly, Mrs. Abercrombie, and Bent Candy, the Baptist deacon. Mr. Powelly is indifferent to the prairie and to how it affects the lives of his congregation. In the middle of a severe drought, with all the crops browned and ruined and people's very survival at stake, Mr. Powelly draws the blinds in the house and composes a sermon on "The Vital Things," using the image of the vine whose branches will be withered if a person is not faithful. His indifference flames into hatred towards the Ben (the Young Ben's father), who epitomizes the prairie's wild freedom, because the latter has outwitted him by pretending conversion in order that he may keep his liquor still secretly in the church basement. Following the hilarious explosion of the still in the middle of divine service, "The minister was aware of an undying, Old Testament thirst for revenge—a thirst, he resolved fiercely, which should have its full slaking one day."

Mr. Powelly is interested in much more than justice, and Mrs. Abercrombie, filled with the same zeal, is his strong right arm. As head of the school board she tries to have the Young Ben sent to reform school, but after years of having her own way in everything, she is defeated and forced into resigning. Bent Candy is a profiteer who buys up dried-out land cheap from ruined farmers. By a strange turn of luck, his land seems to get rain when the others' doesn't. In his greed to own Saint Sammy's Clydesdale horses, he buys the land they graze on and threatens Sammy with expulsion unless he sells the horses. Fortunately, he receives his comeuppance at last when a whirlwind destroys his new barn and ruins his crops. Bent Candy's values are distorted: for example, he is completely uninterested in helping Brian's uncle Sean with his good irrigation scheme because his mind is on other things of greater importance, such as whether the new minister should be allowed to use the Moffat translation of the Bible. These people—Powelly, Abercrombie, and Candy—represent the city as a wilderness of bigotry and self-interest. Saint Sammy has it right when he says of them,

> "Their eyes ain't seen the majesty of His glory ner yet the greatnessa His work, but their ways is before Him an' cannot be hid." Sammy's arm with its hand clawed, lifted, and pointed out the town low on the horizon. "Fer they have played the harlot an' the fornicator in the sighta the Lord!...An' there is sorra an' sighin' over the facea the prairie—herb an' the seed thereof thirsteth after the water which don't cometh! The cutworm cutteth—the rust rusteth an' the 'hopper hoppeth!'"

The Ben and his family are the asocial side of the prairie, at times anti-social. The Ben spends all his money on drink, urinates in the street, and runs a prosperous but illegal still. Not everyone hates the Ben—in the pub he is very popular—but some, like Judge Mortimer, are hypocrites. The judge buys liquor from the Ben, yet sentences him to jail for keeping the still. The Young Ben is indifferent to school, takes holidays when it suits him, and spends his school time looking out at the prairie through the window. He makes no friends except Brian, and seldom speaks to anyone.

The two moderates who sympathize with the Young Ben and try to help are the school principal, Mr. Digby, and the new teacher, Miss Thompson. Digby understands the boy's desire for freedom and his feeling of being caged at school. He pays for the rifle the Young Ben steals, knowing how badly he wants it, and he dismisses him from school a year early. Digby recognizes in Brian something of the same spirit as in the Young Ben, and is the only one in whom Brian confides about "the feeling." Miss Thompson also sympathizes with the Young Ben and tries to relieve his school time as much as she can. Bravely she puts her job on the line to support Digby with the school board, and in doing so brings about the fall from power of Mrs. Abercrombie.

Brian's grandmother is a wilderness person, a homesteader, who has come to live with her daughter's family. She tells Brian and his younger brother, Bobbie, how her husband could fiddle the sounds of the wilderness: the gopher squeaking, crows calling, jack rabbits bouncing. In her last days she can still bring back the smell of the willow on the bank. As Brian grows older his relationship with his grandmother deepens; it is she whom he resembles more than any other person.

Sean, the cursing, hot-tempered uncle, is, as Mitchell says, "the keeper of the Lord's Vineyard, literally." He is a man with a message about irrigation and the sowing of crops, but his words go unheeded. In his anger at the deaf ears around him, he cries out his condemnation in suitably updated biblical style: "'An' what you say is stupid!' roared Sean. 'Threefold stupid fer threefold stupid reasons! A—hen manure! B—heifer dust! C—buffalo chips!'" Sean is no model for wilderness life, even though he manages to create a viable garden. He will teach Brian all he knows, though, and Brian will accomplish what Sean has been trying to do, if it is accomplished at all.

Finally, there is Saint Sammy, the crazy old man driven off his land by crop failures, living in the wilderness in a piano box, with his Clydes, and the voice of the Lord ringing in his ears. He's the parodic version of Sean, another Jeremiah. "'An' the voicea the Lord come ontuh me, sayin', "I kin do the drouthin' out an' the hailin' out an' the 'hopperin' out an' the blowin' out till Bent Candy gits good an' tired out!'" If divinity has a role in this novel at all, it is clearly more on the side of Saint Sammy than on that of the Baptist deacon or the Presbyterian minister.

Brian is the only one who can live truly with the wilderness, neither in it nor entirely out of it. He is planning to be a "dirt doctor," to bring in a new strain of wheat, to teach new methods of irrigation after he has studied at the university. He is also the one who recognizes the eternal, implacable nature of the prairie, the freedom of the wind that people can never share. Because he knows these things and continues to search for the true meaning of all life, he can perhaps make a start at refertilizing the wilderness.

Who Has Seen the Wind was written 55 years ago, *Henderson* about ten years later. They remain as fresh, as ardently persuasive as if they had been written today. But no one would write them today. No one dares, because the present time will not permit us to believe in such large, imaginative souls as Brian or Henderson. People do not write novels about characters with that combination of personal power, insight, and the urge to truth that would enable them to change anything in the world— just any one thing—for good. (I'm not talking about slush fiction, or pathetic revivals of Prince Valiant or Jack Armstrong the All-American Boy.) Today's heroes struggle, as have several we have looked at, with integrity and futility just to survive. Gregor, the Swede, *Surfacing*'s hero, the dog King are among them. Ruby and Ada, too, but Inman doesn't even get that far. The people of Wiebe's tale, while some of them would qualify, are from another time. Milton's "patience and heroic martyrdom" seem to be today's stance, or the old war cry of grin and bear it. Except that most of them aren't grinning.

As I finish rereading what I have written, I am sitting in an old stone cottage on the west coast of Galway, in a bay facing Inishturk and Achill islands and the ocean. We have had three days of wind, rain, and fog, as the clouds blow at us, lowering, growing faint, opening a shred to let a gleam of sun come through, then folding themselves over it again and dimming the view. The wind blows down the chimney of our small cottage, but the peat fire draws it up again. With an insouciance that I am beginning to think reflects an Irish approach to living, the owner has put in thermopane windows, but has not thought to caulk the chinks between the roof and the walls. Energy saved is more than matched by energy wasted, and the room is pervasively chilled. We consume gallons of tea, which, strangely, seems to work better than coffee. The Irish know a thing or two about keeping the insides warm, the other thing or two being Jameson's and Guinness.

For fireside pleasure I am reading some Irish poets, spurred on by Seamus Heaney's writings about them. I discover these marvellous lines, the quotation of the day—perhaps of the year, who knows, the lifetime—

of Patrick Kavanagh's: "For this soul needs to be honoured with a new dress woven/From green and blue things and arguments that cannot be proven."[28]

There. There's the mystic side of the wilderness process I am investigating, through mind and soul, and especially body these days, when the weather impinges for good or ill on the other parts. Weather is a strong contender here, in this chilly damp, this soft rain guided by the controlling wind, so severe sometimes that I can hardly walk upright on a sloping path. Through this the poet's lovely pulse comes and overcomes, beating lyrically despite the weather. Or does it happen because of the weather?

For this is another sort of wilderness, this tempestuous seaside with its distant land masses appearing and vanishing, ghostly humped gray forms coming through the fog. And through it the voice of the poet speaks truth. I am like Inman, wanting all things to be in right order, sun above, blue sky and green mountains, shimmering loughs. Then I will have my insights, hear my good voices, learn the new songs. Kavanagh's lines read in this soggy, indistinct landscape tell me that these voices come in the real wilderness, not the one I put to rights first. Henderson's voice came through heat and horrors; mine seems to be slinking through the boggy, foggy dew. How dreadful to contemplate—the possibility that soul discoveries may come at the worst (or the least comfortable) of times, and not in the full sun of my garden in May.

Kavanagh's lines are just what I need and partially know. I am torn between looking for the new dress and putting up arguments to include it. I'm no Brian. Such alternating between symbolic fact and theory produces irony in me, a handy position, but one I'm growing tired of. The poet tells me to give up trying to defend a position and to revel in being. (No, I'm absolutely not going to try and say what that means. That's ultimately what I need to discover in my wilderness sojourns.)

Today's last irony: the wilderness I see in front of me appears through the wide double-glazed window. It's not Plato's cave, but still an invisible screen holding me away from reality.

10

— THE WILDERNESS SHALL BLOOM AGAIN —

Let the wilderness and the dry lands exult,
let the wasteland rejoice and bloom,
let it bring forth flowers like the jonquil,
let it rejoice and sing for joy....
Then the eyes of the blind shall be opened,
the ears of the deaf unsealed,
then the lame shall leap like a deer
and the tongues of the dumb sing for joy....

Isaiah 35:1-2, 5-6

The condition of man's relation to God is first of all one of not having, not seeing, not knowing, and not grasping.

Paul Tillich, "Waiting"

What any true painting touches is an absence—an absence of which, without the painting, we might be unaware. And that would be our loss. The painter's continual search is for a place to welcome the absent. If he finds a place, he arranges it and prays for the face of the absent to appear.

John Berger, "Studio Talk"

When God is about to turn the earth into a paradise he does not begin his work where there is some good growth already, but in the wilderness, where nothing grows, and nothing is to be seen but dry sand and rocks; that the light may shine out of darkness, the world be replenished from emptiness, and the earth watered by springs from a droughty desert.

Jonathan Edwards, "The Latter-Day Glory Is Probably to Begin in America"

I n the end, it all comes down to Isaiah.

The images of the wilderness form a narrative. At the beginning there is the Exodus, separating the faithful from the recalcitrant, threatening death to the latter, a new covenant to the former. We see the scapegoat thrown out as a way of purifying the community. Then the prophets escape into the wilderness, and return with their messages of condemnation or promise. The people waste the land, they become vile, and the prophets tell of worse punishments to come. A new prophet comes into the wilderness to tell of the coming of the Messiah. Jesus is sent into the wilderness, where he is tested and returns to preach the good news.

You could wind up here, taking Jesus through his own wilderness of abandonment and crucifixion, and ending with his resurrection. I would have made the expected theological point, but in doing so I would have falsified the evidence. Look about you: is this not some kind of wilderness life we are in? Read these books: are they not telling us something rather akin to what the biblical writers were saying?

The story the wilderness tells does not end with an event, but with a promise. Isaiah says to a beleaguered people not to give up hope, because some day the wilderness itself will be changed, both the one we live in and the one that lives in us.

I looked about for recent books, even just one, that had taken on this bountiful image as either setting or promise, while at the same time keeping us in a believable fictional structure and a believable present. (Tolkien's universe, while very much to the point here, is just not ours.) There may be one, but I haven't found it. I toyed briefly with the idea of taking on the task myself, of attempting to answer this question: How could Isaiah's prophecy be believed today, and how could we begin to fulfill it? I wouldn't dare to attempt it.

I was left with the books I've been considering for some time now. Do they have any hints, any indications as to how Isaiah's words might come into being? Of course they do. Once I had got it out of my head that the answers to the question wouldn't come out of the blue but out of lived experience, then I could see it easily. This is, of course, what the wilderness is there for: you go into it in order to see. How had I missed the main point all along?

In turning back to the literature again, collecting seeds that might sprout and refresh the dry land, I must warn you about what to expect and what will be absent. For instance, for every writer who illustrates the wilderness of the mind, there is a theologian somewhere, or a concerned social activist, or a scientist, who will tell us that the whole world is a wilderness and we'd better work on that instead. For every writer who introduces us to an individual struggling to be born, there are theologians and social critics who will say that the only way to make a straight path through the wilderness is by laying it down together.

Novels are about private lives; plays, for the most part, are too. When the world is going to (bad) seed, privacy seems an old-fashioned luxury. Yet we must start somewhere. Mind cleanup comes first; then we can see straight in order to lay level paths. Of course this thought is utopian, too. We'll never see straight all together. The world is full of thin, nervous people hiding in shadows or behind tinted glasses. The writers I've chosen to write about do see something clearly of the past, the present. They can be counted on to have a few clues about what it takes to make a possible blooming future.

Here are some of the ways by which the wilderness can be made to bloom again.

Listening and looking. All the characters in these works who are changing, moving towards a future they never anticipated, have their senses tuned to the animate and inanimate world around them. Brian hears the wind, Henderson takes on the bearing of the lioness, Pierre sees his mountain. It is the island itself that gives Mary Lamb the encouragement to continue with her writing:

> Mary felt the instant fasten round her, fit her, inside and out; finally, massively, shockingly articulate. This one shrug of blood, valved in her heart; this one taste of breath, its fractions of sea rock, grasses, earth, a note of honeysuckle, a note of pine; this one black and dove sky, flesh hot; this one lighthouse twitch; this one blink of absolute comfort when she started to stretch, to swallow and then *know* this one exponential scream of unconfined generosity, possibility, life. It changed her mind.

Surfacing's "I" undergoes an extreme version of the same discovery that the natural world can alter one's life radically when she has her underwater vision.

It was below me, drifting towards me from the furthest level where there was no life, a dark oval trailing limbs. It was blurred but it had eyes, they were open, it was something I knew about, a dead thing, it was dead.

This is the beginning of the restoration of her memory of her abortion and the beginning of a new life, head and heart now rejoined.

Theologian Rosemary Radford Ruether seems to understand this process when she writes:

We need to take the time to sit under trees, look at water, and at the sky, observe small biotic communities of plants and animals with close attention, get back in touch with the living earth. We can start to release the stifled intuitive and creative powers of our organism, to draw and to write poetry, and to know that we stand on holy ground.[29]

Remembering. This is what kept the Hebrews going during their 40-year ordeal. This is how the prophets encouraged them during the Exile and the Babylonian captivity: remember how God sustained and led our ancestors through the wilderness. Religions, no matter which one, depend on memory for survival.

I have stood several times in the midst of the cemetery at Arles in France, called Alyscamps, the Elysian Fields. Here are empty stone sarcophagi, which have held different occupants over the centuries since their pre-Roman construction. The people who used to inhabit these tombs wanted to be remembered, but their bodies were not left in peace; even their names were effaced by subsequent communities and over time. One of the purposes of the Nazi death camps in assigning numbers to the prisoners was to erase the names of those they interred and killed, so no one would ever find them again, or remember them. The poor also leave no memory of themselves behind. Vico's and Vica's stories of their former lives die with them.

Memory is not always liberating. Dwelling in the past, with nostalgia, anger, or guilt, and never putting finish to them, is a way of avoiding change. Nagg and Nell, Hamm's parents in *Endgame*, have only the recollections of a happier past to keep them going. Hamm, on the other hand, wants to obliterate memory and have done with the whole game of living. Nathan Staples lives a good deal of his time in memory, thinking longingly about his ex-wife, Maura. Only after a sequence of nasty shocks, and through the growing affection of his daughter Mary, does he abandon the memories. The book he has written about them is finished.

Denial of the past is also a hindrance to growth. The Swede's wife, Dawn, excludes all nastiness from her memory, and never speaks of her daughter. Swede, on the other hand, thinks back constantly to the times when Merry was still with them, asking himself, did I do wrong? What else could I have done? Michael Berg, in *The Reader*, asks himself the same questions about his affair with Hanna. Rayber, one of the most distraught characters in this collection, has tried to wipe out the memory of his uncle Mason's words; now, with the coming of Tarwater, his fury seems "to be stirring from buried depths that had lain quiet for years and to be working upward, closer and closer, toward the slender roots of his peace." Not even the revival of his memory will save Rayber, lost soul that he is.

Memory of home and Ada keeps Inman going, and although he dies in the end, he is one of the most hopeful and realistic characters in this group of wilderness sojourners. Tribal memory plays an integral part in the life of the Tetsot'ine. The memory of the mountain is what gives Pierre his vocation as an artist, to paint for others. In *Surfacing*, of course, the restoration of the hero's memory is central to the whole process of renewal.

Questioning. Our books, and the characters in them, because they are located in the wilderness, raise more questions than they answer. That's why you go to the wilderness in the first place, most of the time. If you knew it all, you wouldn't be there. The "Who am I?" and the "Where is here?" questions are at the forefront. Less noticeable, often implied, but still lurking on the sidelines in some of this literature, is the question of God—character, presence, behaviour.

The Tetsot'ine are the first characters to suggest that the creation story is a great mistake and that we are its victims. Keskarrah's comment, "Their first story tells them everything is always wrong. So wherever they go, they can see only how wrong the world is," makes the reader want to look again at the Whitemud tale. Inman's view of the world carries on the theodicy question: "I wouldn't want," he says, "to puzzle too long about the why of pain nor the frame of mind somebody would be in to make up a thing like it to begin with." He cannot imagine having "deep faith in right order…when it was in such short supply." In *King*, Vico carries Inman's view a bit further:

Only God can help. I tell him this with my eyes.
There are places God doesn't come to.
The terrain?
No. Here. He points his finger like a gun at his own temple.

When King says to Vico, "The world is so bad, God has to exist," Vico replies, "Most people...would draw the opposite conclusion."

The Orator as a parody of God in *Les Chaises* is clearly helpless, while in *Endgame* God is either non-existent or parodied in the character of Hamm. In a decidedly non-ironic vein are Gregor's questions in *The Gates of the Forest*: Where is the Messiah? Will he come? Has he come?

In none of these ideas do we find any sense of the God of the wilderness as teaching, comforting or, for that matter, even punishing. Evil seems to be gratuitous and undeserved, and the love of God is not suggested for a minute. Still, the questions about God that are implied in these books require answers.

In thinking about the Holocaust, I ask whether we must say that God died at Auschwitz, that God was indeed with the Jews as they were slaughtered, in truth and in being. But the world goes on, which God has made and kept alive. Without God there is no world whatsoever. So we can in one way say that God has been resurrected—in our lives, and in the world altogether. That is one possible way to rethink it. Certainly after World War II we cannot imagine God in the same way. There was no justice for those who worshipped him, whom God had chosen long ago. The promise was not kept. The sword did go through the land, and the Jews could not lie down quietly and not be afraid. There is no imperial He, dispensing punishment to the wicked and testing his chosen. Auschwitz was neither punishment nor test. But God is not responsible for it, either. There is no grand plan where all who suffered will be seen to have participated in an overall redemptive scheme, a new land or a new Jerusalem. The problem of evil has not been explained. Nor has the problem of being, the nature of the relationship between God and the world.

Understanding. While coming to recognize the truth of the world we live in isn't enough to bring it into bloom, without understanding there is no beginning of change. One of the loveliest attempts is made by Robert Hood and Greenstockings, whose affection for each other urges them to learn as best they can about their strange and almost opposite worlds. In an equally brief time at the end of his life, Pierre's life is enriched by his discovery that the art he had kept to himself could serve the world.

Not all understanding of how the world really turns brings joy or satisfaction, however. When the Swede's self-constructed American pastoral falls apart, he is left a hollow shell with a cleanly scrubbed façade. He knows this, but it doesn't help. Gregor, who decides to try and rescue his failing marriage with Clara, understands that "[w]hether or not the Messiah comes doesn't matter; we'll manage without him." The agonizing questions have been resolved to some extent, but for Gregor the road ahead is not strewn with flowers.

To refuse to look and question and come to understand is to lose your chance at real life. Hanna is the clearest example here of what denial can do to you. To save herself embarrassment, she will spend a much longer time in prison than if she had admitted that she couldn't write. To re-enter the world seems to her to be unthinkable, so she commits suicide. The Old Man and the Old Woman live—and die—in denial. What to think of Nathan—after his last bits of psychodrama, is he finished with staging his life, and has he begun to participate in the everyday world? That seems to be the way he is headed, but the author is silent here. Henderson has certainly learned a great deal, but what he does with it is anybody's guess.

Compassion. The next step that follows spiritually after understanding is compassion. Thomas Merton sees it as a true wilderness:

> There is no wilderness so terrible, so beautiful, so arid, and so fruitful as the wilderness of compassion. It is the only desert that will truly flourish like the lily. It shall become a pool. It shall bud forth and blossom and rejoice with joy. It is in the desert of compassion that the thirsty land turns into springs of water, that the poor possess all things.[30]

What stands out in my mind about the books considered here is the distinct lack of compassion in most of them. In fact, this lack is one of the most visible qualities of some of the chief characters. Think of Rayber, Hamm, Nichole, Michael in *The Reader*. In other books it is the lack of compassion on the part of others that puts the hero in a tough situation. There are all the nasties who make Inman's return home so difficult; there are those who come to evict the squatters in *King*; and the villagers who condemn Cristina. There is the father of the narrator's child in *Surfacing*, now recalled to mind, and David and Anna, who see the strung-up bird as a good photo op.

Despite the prevailing sense that the world has turned cold, vicious, or indifferent, signs of compassion appear in the most unlikely places. Orok the hunter rescues Pierre in Ungava; Hood sees compassion in the family of Birdseye; Miss Thompson and Mr. Digby rescue Brian's friend the Young Ben. Mary Lamb's gay "uncles" have it, as do the great women of the Arnewi tribe whom Henderson tries to help. Finally, it is Henderson himself who has my vote for the one most likely to grow into a fuller expression of compassion, followed closely by Brian the potential "dirt doctor."

Refusing. In a world that seems profane, there are heroic and not-so-heroic ways of refusing to live that way. We see it most directly when Tarwater rejects the pleasant stranger with the devilish-sounding suggestions. We watch the narrator in *Surfacing* gradually discovering David's and Anna's phony and abusive attitudes to the world and finally rejecting them. Miss Thompson, Brian's teacher in *Who Has Seen the Wind*, refuses to submit to the plans of the pseudo-religious school board members.

There are other chief characters whose actions are more ambiguous. Nichole, the crippled girl in *The Sweet Hereafter*, puts the blame for the bus accident on Dolores as a way of gaining a hold over her abusive father. Her refusal to tell the truth about how the accident happened is entirely an act of vengeance, since in her changed condition she knows she will not have any more physical attention from her father. She has made her own situation better, but no one else's. Then there is Merry, whose rash action tries to draw attention to a war she and many others condemned. Having killed by accident, she goes on to set other bombs that she knows will kill. Then, having refused in this violent way to accept the American ideology, she takes up the way of non-violence. At best one could say she is a failed hero, and even that is probably not part of the book's intention.

Several characters are notable for their refusal to be victims. Vico confronts the guard trying to evict the squatters, an act as noble as it is foolish. Cristina in *Lives of the Saints* leaves her village calling down curses on the hypocritical, unforgiving citizens who have lined up to watch her leave. "You are the ones who are dead, not me," she cries, "because not one of you knows what it means to be free and to make a choice...!" Still, she is not free either, caught between a lover and a husband. She does not live long enough to discover that perhaps she is still a victim. Dolores is of course a visible victim who cannot do much about it except resign herself to a different kind of life. Her refusal to be a victim to herself comes through her knowledge that Nichole has lied—something that only she and the lawyer Mitchell know. She is what theologian Elizabeth Johnson calls a "holy survivor."[31]

Finally, three of the authors deserve to be celebrated for their refusal to play the game: Wiesel, Berger, and Beckett. In the first two it is the theme, the action, the intent of their novels to condemn a world grown cruel, indifferent and heartless towards those it victimizes or excludes. Beckett tosses his whole fictional world into a profane parody of the sacred, offering no fictional alternative—only our understanding of this bleak world might make the difference, perhaps.

Coming together. Wilderness people have the potential to abandon the old ways of being together and to grow as a group. Wiebe shows the separateness and the tentative new growth in understanding between Franklin's party and the Tetsot'ine. (Outside this fictional world, we know it was a failed experiment, but that doesn't matter here.) At the end of Cold Mountain a new group has formed, from which the old animosity and indifference between Ruby and Stobrod has disappeared. As many of the characters in Everything You Need drop their hostility and false assumptions about each other and their neediness ceases to cry out so loudly, there is the possibility of a loving, stimulating community in the making. Even in King, although the squatters are gathered together out of need, they demonstrate kindness and thoughtfulness that go beyond just self-survival. These novels suggest that perhaps there is a chance for human community; up till now I had thought that the only good communities were made up of rabbits or hobbits.

Going up the mountain. Not everyone can find a mountain to listen to, metaphorically speaking. By this I mean searching out or being driven into a quiet place to discover what your heart most desires, or, another way, what is required of you. In the varied characters who seek a mountain experience, the impulse comes sometimes from within, sometimes from beyond them. Pierre's is an interior urgency, as is Henderson's; in both cases the medium, the "voice" they discover, comes from outside, from mountain and lion. The mysterious Gavriel acts as the recuperative voice for Gregor, left helplessly alone in the forest. The narrator in *Surfacing* doesn't even know she has something to learn; she believes that she is riven, head from heart, and that nothing will change. Yet she searches for a message from her father, and instead, discovers how she may reconnect herself. Brian goes to the prairie because it is there. He has no longing, no voice calling him. He is simply a child who is ready and able to see and hear. As a hilarious example of a failed attempt at going up the mountain, there is Joe Christopher's theory that after seven near-death experiences, the truth of the universe will be revealed. In one of these attempts, Eckless the dog nearly dies, and Nathan swears off trying.

Becoming. Rosemary Radford Ruether says that there are two ways to begin to change society. One is by forming a model community to be a light for the world—my ancestor's city on the hill. The other is to create new forms of organization to meet particular, urgent needs. Scaling this vision down in size, but not in importance, novels offer also two possibilities for becoming new, in communal groups and as individuals. We have already looked at the community as it works its way through the wilderness. Now we shall see how the wilderness sojourners in these novels become what they choose to be or what they must be.

This is the winners' circle only. Not all of our heroes made it. Some of them could not or would not find a path, or manna to feed them, or a voice to urge them on. My votes for Becomers on their way to Be-ers are, in no ranking order, Henderson, who sees the wilderness as his only hope of rescue, and who learns, as he tells us, by blows. There is Nathan, who also learns by blows, and for whom the wilderness began as a needed shelter, but is rapidly becoming home—a very unbiblical idea. For Gregor the forest wilderness is a last resort, a kind of dead end, until he is rescued by others. He is reviving at the end of the novel by accepting the new world as he finds it, without mentors or Messiah.

Tarwater is finished with the wilderness and his past life. He has accepted his role as prophet and is going towards the city to call for its repentance. Inman travels through the wilderness, which is both shelter and a necessary evil that he hates. His characteristic hopefulness keeps him going, and his hope is rewarded at the end, if only briefly. King, too, is one who hopes. He takes the wilderness as it is, but in his fantasy at the end of the book where he believes he is rescuing the people, we see how unfounded his hopes are.

Two more characters who die, Hood and Pierre, are able to use the wilderness for a well. Hood enters into it joyfully through his love for Greenstockings, although it kills him in the end. Pierre comes to see his mountain as holy, and the vision enriches the rest of his life.

The final three characters who are becoming more and more what they mean to be, and for whom the wilderness is the catalyst, are Mary Lamb, the narrator of *Surfacing*, and Brian O'Connal. All three see the wilderness as a beautiful and important part of their lives. All three have learned from it lessons about love, cruelty, sadness, and pain. Implicit in all the novels in which these characters appear is that place and person are connected, soul to soul, and that the relationship is a sacred one. It makes one want to be, as Steiner says, a "gambler on transcendence."[32]

After I had written all the foregoing, I came back, with urgings from my friends, to ask myself what Jesus once asked the crowd: What did you go out into the wilderness to see? What did I expect, and what did I find? I came expecting to tell you what I know about others' visions. I did that, but through the writing or perhaps through the spaces, the not-quite-certain parts, came the questions, Hamm's "all the old questions."

First is the one I began with: Where is here? The answer is far too complex to be undertaken even by a walloping great assemblage of storytellers such as we've met here. They do their best. In every century I'm sure there have been diehard answers to Frye's question. Under the pressure of new knowledge, new circumstances, new moral contexts, they have come to smithereens, like a sort of little-bang explosion of the world, only to be replaced by other certainties due to blow up in their turn. Still, the question expands like a gas to fill the space left vacant.

To make my own feeble attempt at a response—hardly an answer—I call on the one metaphorical idea that lurks and rumbles its way through-out this book: the movement that brings the wilderness into the mind, and the mind to the wilderness. So if you will, imagine me walking through a wilderness early in the morning, when the mist still covers the land, going carefully and very quietly in case I might disturb some living creature, or bang my shins on a too-solid rock. Once in a while I fall over a root, muttering the usual expletives and giving forth wails of misery. As the daylight comes up, it is possible to see a little in front of me. I can avoid the shrubs and the small stumbly stuff and make a sort of pathway. The mist thins, and I begin to see shapes further away—the odd tree, a heap of stones, perhaps even a moving being. I keep walking, but because there are no co-ordinates and no horizon, I don't know if the land is rising or falling or just staying flatly the same. Because my balance is poor, I trip a lot. Suddenly, all at once, quick as a snake, the mist is scooped away and I find myself in an actual setting—the top of a hill surrounded by circling birds, or a patch of clover-dotted meadow, or a marshy place holding up a cluster of cattails. Every glimpse through the mist is a wonder, like a small bead swinging alone, invisibly attached to the great thread of meaning. Do these threads make up a canopy to encompass the world? Sometimes I think they do, but I cannot see it. The mist encloses me again, and I plod on.

Writing this book has caused me to see these breaks in the mist of uncertainty for the holy things they are. Tillich's words at the beginning of this chapter assure me that the mist is part of the waiting, just as the wilderness is the place where the waiting goes on, which is the greater part of becoming what we are to be.

The other questions that are mine, and perhaps yours, are these: Does the wilderness matter? Will it bloom again? To the first I reply, emphatically, yes; to the second, it's a gamble.

Reading and writing and thinking about the wilderness for so long has slowed me down, although I am still hungry, tearing away at literature as if it were my last meal. Like the Hebrews on a good manna day, I want to gobble it all up, and save the leftovers in case I should run out tomorrow—or there's no tomorrow. Still, I have begun to take time to do as Ruether suggests, to read poetry, even write a little, and to try and discover what Yeats calls "the spiritual intellect's great work."[33] That's a very good start.

This excursion into the wilderness has given me real ground on which to stand. I hated being alone with my rambling thoughts and sticky questions. Here in this corner of the literary universe I am among friends. They and I don't all agree with each other, but we do all believe that the wilderness matters, that without it life would be one-dimensional, locked-in, footbound, not footloose. We know that the old questions require new answers, which may not exist yet—or ever.

Some writers, probably only a few, might believe that the wilderness will bloom again. If so, they are there to point the way. Most, myself included, leave the answer in doubt. (Isaiah's listeners would have thought the same.) I cannot of course speak for these writers, but I like to assume that they give the wilderness a good chance of being refertilized. Otherwise, why write about it? Like John Berger's painter, one tries to find a place to welcome the absent, and prays for the face of the absent to appear—the absent, which is on its way, although we do not know it.

> ...for still
> I am a willow in the wilderness,
> Loving the wind that bent me.

Emerson, "Musketaquid"

— NOTES —

1 H.A. Williams, *The True Wilderness* (London: Constable, 1965), 30-31.

2 Henry David Thoreau, *Walden and Other Writings* (Toronto: Bantam, 1982), 339.

3 *Figaro Magazine*, 20 avril 2002.

4 Terry L. Burden, *The Kerygma of the Wilderness Traditions in the Hebrew Bible* (New York: Peter Lang, 1994), 197.

5 Melvin Charney, *Parables and Other Allegories: The Work of Melvin Charney 1975–1990* (Montreal: Canadian Centre for Architecture, 1991), 128.

6 Simon P. Sibelman, *Silence in the Novels of Elie Wiesel* (New York: St. Martin's Press, 1995), 31.

7 Lawrence L. Langer, *The Holocaust and the Literary Imagination* (New Haven, CT: Yale University Press, 1975), 91.

8 "À la limite, il appartient à Gavriel de s'identifier. S'il choisit de ne rien dire, Grégor pourrait peut-être s'exprimer à sa place." *Tous les fleuves vont à la mer.* Paris: Éditions du Seuil, 1994, p. 483.

9 Primo Levi, *The Drowned and the Saved* (New York: Vintage, 1989), 70.

10 George Steiner, *No Passion Spent* (New Haven, CT: Yale University Press, 1996), 342.

11 Levi, *The Drowned and the Saved*, 27.

12 George Steiner, *Language and Silence* (New Haven, CT: Yale University Press, 1998), 150.

13 Erna Paris, *Long Shadows: Truth, Lies and History* (Toronto: Alfred A. Knopf, 2000), 40.

14 *Ibid.*, p. 85.

15 George Steiner, *In Bluebeard's Castle: Some Notes Towards the Re-definition of Culture* (London: Faber & Faber, 1971), 51.

16 Charney, *Parables and Other Allegories*, 128.

17 Levi, *The Drowned and the Saved*, 106.

18 Steiner, *In Bluebeard's Castle*, 57.

19 Jacques Ellul in Darrell J. Fasching, *Narrative Theology after Auschwitz* (Atlanta: Scholars Press, 1999), 12.

20 Langer, *The Holocaust and the Literary Imagination*, 76.

21 Elie Wiesel in Ekkehard Schuster & Reinhold Boschert-Kimmig, *Hope Against Hope: Johann Baptist Metz and Elie Wiesel Speak out on the Holocaust* (New York: Paulist Press, 1999), 76.

22 Rosemary Radford Ruether, *Faith and Fratricide: The Theological Roots of Anti-Semitism* (Eugene, OR: Wipf and Stock Publishers, 1997), 224.

23 John Milton, *Paradise Lost* IX 31-32; XII, 587.

24 Elizabeth A. Johnson, *Friends of God and Prophets* (Ottawa: Novalis, 1998), 17.

25 F.W. Danker in Joachim Jeremias, *New Testament Theology* (London: SCM Press, 1971), 112.

26 Flannery O'Connor, *The Habit of Being*, ed. Sally Fitzgerald (New York: Farrar Straus Giroux, 1979), 350.

27 Belden C. Lane, *The Solace of Fierce Landscapes* (New York: Oxford University Press, 1998), 17.

28 Patrick Kavanagh, "Canal Bank Walk," in *Selected Poems* (London: Penguin Books, 2000), 126.

29 Rosemary Radford Ruether, *Gaia and God: An Ecofeminist Theology of Earth Healing* (San Francisco: HarperCollins, 1992), 271.

30 *The Intimate Merton: His Life from His Journals*, ed. Patrick Hart and Jonathan Montaldo. San Francisco: HarperSanFrancisco, 1999, p. 86.

31 Johnson, *Friends of God and Prophets*, 155.

32 Steiner, *In Bluebeard's Castle*, 71.

33 W.B. Yeats, "The Man and the Echo," in *Collected Poems of W.B. Yeats* (London: MacMillan &Co., 1965), 394.

— WORKS CONSULTED —

Aaron, Soazig. *Le Non de Klara*. Maurice Nadeau, 2002.

Anderson, Bernhard W. *Understanding the Old Testament*. Englewood Cliffs, NJ: Prentice-Hall, 1957.

Atwood, Margaret. *Strange Things: The Malevolent North in Canadian Literature*. Oxford: Clarendon Press, 1995.

———. *Surfacing*. Toronto: McClelland and Stewart, 1972.

Banks, Russell. *The Sweet Hereafter*. Toronto: Vintage Canada, 1991.

Beckett, Samuel. *Endgame*. New York: Grove Press, 1958.

Bellow, Saul. *Henderson the Rain King*. New York: Fawcett Publications, 1959.

Berenbaum, Michael. *The Vision of the Void: Theological Reflections on the Works of Elie Wiesel*. Middletown, CT: Wesleyan University Press, 1979.

Berger, John. *King: A Street Story*. New York: Vintage, 1999.

———. "Studio Talk," in *Miquel Barceló 1987–1997*, ed. Pep Subirós. Barcelona: Museu d'Art Contemporani de Barcelona, 1998.

Bonnard, Pierre. "La signification du désert selon le Nouveau Testament," in *Hommage et Reconnaissance*. Neuchâtel: Delachaux & Niestle, 1946.

Bremer, Francis J. *Shaping New Englands: Puritan Clergymen in Seventeenth-Century England and New England*. Don Mills, ON: Macmillan, 1994.

Burden, Terry L. *The Kerygma of the Wilderness Traditions in the Hebrew Bible*. New York: Peter Lang, 1994.

Charney, Melvin. *Parables and Other Allegories: The Work of Melvin Charney 1975–1990*. Montreal: Canadian Centre for Architecture, 1991.

Cherry, Conrad, ed. *God's New Israel*. Chapel Hill, NC: University of North Carolina Press, 1998.

Dostoevsky, Fyodor. *The Karamazov Brothers*. Oxford: Oxford University Press, 1994.

Eckardt, A. Roy with Alice L. Eckardt, *Long Night's Journey into Day: Life and Faith after the Holocaust*. Detroit: Wayne State University Press, 1982.

Eliot, T.S. *Collected Poems 1909–1935*. London: Faber and Faber, 1949.

————. *The Cocktail Party*. London: Faber and Faber, 1950.

Fasching, Darrell J. *Narrative Theology after Auschwitz*. Atlanta, GA: Scholars Press, 1999.

Fine, Ellen S. *Legacy of Night: The Literary Universe of Elie Wiesel*. Albany, NY: SUNY Press, 1982.

Frazier, Charles. *Cold Mountain*. Toronto: Vintage Canada, 1998.

French, Allen. *Historic Concord*. Ipswich: Concord Free Public Library, 1978.

Frye, Northrop. *The Bush Garden: Essays on the Canadian Imagination*. Toronto: House of Anansi Press, 1971.

Green, Hannah. *I Never Promised You a Rose Garden*. New York: New American Library, 1964.

Greenberg, Rabbi Irving. *The Jewish Way: Living the Holidays*. New York: Simon & Schuster, 1988.

Groover, Kristina K. *The Wilderness Within: American Women Writers and Spiritual Quest*. Fayetteville: University of Arkansas Press, 1999.

Guillet, Jacques. *Themes of the Bible*. Notre Dame, IN: Fides, 1965.

Hart, Albert Bushnell, ed. *Commonwealth History of Massachusetts*, vol. 1. New York: Russell & Russell, 1966.

Ionesco, Eugène. *Les Chaises*, in *Théâtre 1*. Éditions Gallimard, 1954.

————. *The Chairs*. In *Three Plays*, tr. Donald Watson, London: John Calder, 1963.

Jacobs, Steven L., ed. *Contemporary Christian Religious Responses to the Shoah.* New York: University Press of America, 1993.

Jameson, Anna Brownell. *Winter Studies and Summer Rambles in Canada.* Toronto: McClelland & Stewart, 1990.

Jeremias, Joachim. *New Testament Theology*, Vol. 1. London: SCM Press, 1971.

Johnson, Edward. *Wonder-Working Providence of Sions Saviour in New England (1654)* and *Good News from New England (1648).* Delmar, NY: Scholars' Facsimiles & Reprints, Inc., 1974.

Johnson, Elizabeth A. *Friends of God and Prophets: A Feminist Reading of the Communion of Saints.* Ottawa: Novalis, 1998.

Jones, D.G. *Butterfly on Rock.* Toronto: University of Toronto Press, 1973.

Jones, Phyllis M. & Nicholas R., eds. *Salvation in New England: Selections from the Sermons of the First Preachers.* Austin, TX: University of Texas, 1977.

Kavanagh, Patrick. *Selected Poems.* London: Penguin Books, 2000.

Kennedy, A.L. *Everything You Need.* London: Vintage, 2000.

Kittell, Gerhard, ed. *Theological Dictionary of the New Testament*, II, tr. and ed. Geoffrey Bromiley. Grand Rapids, MI: Eerdmans, 1974.

Lane, Belden C. *The Solace of Fierce Landscapes.* New York: Oxford University Press, 1998.

Langer, Lawrence L. *The Holocaust and the Literary Imagination.* New Haven, CT: Yale University Press, 1975.

Levi, Primo. *The Drowned and the Saved*, tr. Raymond Rosenthal. New York: Vintage, 1989.

Malory, Sir Thomas. *Le Morte d'Arthur.* Harmondsworth, Middlesex: Penguin, 1969.

McClintock, James I. *Nature's Kindred Spirits.* Madison, WI: University of Wisconsin Press, 1994.

McClintock, John and James Strong. *Cyclopaedia of Biblical, Theological and Ecclesiastical Literature*. Grand Rapids, MI: Baker Book House, 1968.

McGrath, Robin. *Canadian Inuit Literature: The Development of a Tradition*. Ottawa: National Museums of Canada, 1984.

Merton, Thomas. *The Intimate Merton: His Life from His Journals*, ed. Patrick Hart and Jonathan Montaldo, HarperSanFrancisco, 1999.

Miller, Arthur. *Death of a Salesman*. New York: The Viking Press, 1949.

Milton, John. *The Student's Milton*, New York: Appleton-Century-Crofts, 1933.

Mitchell, W.O. *Who Has Seen the Wind?* Toronto: Macmillan, 1977.

O'Connor, Flannery. *The Habit of Being*, ed. Sally Fitzgerald. New York: Farrar Straus Giroux, 1979.

————. *The Violent Bear it Away*, in 3 *by Flannery O'Connor*. New York: Signet, 1983.

Paris, Erna. *Long Shadows: Truth, Lies and History*. Toronto: Alfred A. Knopf Canada, 2000.

Ricci, Nino. *Lives of the Saints*. Dunvegan, ON: Cormorant Books, 1990.

Roberts-Miller, Patricia. *Voices in the Wilderness: Public Discourse and the Paradox of Puritan Rhetoric*. Tuscaloosa, AL: University of Alabama, 1999.

Roth, Philip. *American Pastoral*. Toronto: Random House of Canada, 1998.

Roy, Gabrielle. *La montagne secrète*. Montréal: Boréal, 1994.

————. *The Hidden Mountain*, tr. Harry Binsse. Toronto: McClelland and Stewart, 1974.

Ruether, Rosemary Radford. *Faith and Fratricide: The Theological Roots of Anti-Semitism*. Eugene, OR: Wipf and Stock Publishers, 1997.

————. *Gaia & God: An Ecofeminist Theology of Earth Healing*. San Francisco: HarperCollins, 1992.

Schama, Simon. *Landscape and Memory*. Toronto: Vintage Canada, 1996.

Schlink, Bernhard. *The Reader*, tr. Carol Brown Janeway. Toronto: Random House of Canada, 1997.

Schneiders, Sandra M. *With Oil in Their Lamps; Faith Feminism, and the Future*. New York: Paulist Press, 2000.

Schuster, Ekkehard & Boschert-Kimmig, Reinhold. *Hope Against Hope: Johann Baptist Metz and Elie Wiesel Speak out on the Holocaust*. New York: Paulist Press, 1999.

Shakespeare, William. *King Lear*. London: Methuen, 1968.

Sibelman, Simon P. *Silence in the Novels of Elie Wiesel*. New York: St. Martin's Press, 1995.

Steele, Michael R. *Christianity, Tragedy, and Holocaust Literature*. Westport, CT: Greenwood Press, 1995.

Steiner, George. *In Bluebeard's Castle: Some Notes Towards the Re-definition of Culture*. London: Faber & Faber, 1971.

———. *Language and Silence*. New Haven, CT: Yale University Press, 1998.

———. *No Passion Spent*. New Haven, CT: Yale University Press, 1996.

The High History of the Holy Grail, tr. Sebastian Evans. London: James Clarke & Co. Ltd., 1969.

The Jerusalem Bible. Garden City, NY: Doubleday, 1968.

The Quest of the Holy Grail, tr. P.M. Matarasso. Harmondsworth: Penguin Books Limited, 1969.

The Romance of Percival in Prose: A Translation of the E Manuscript of the Didot Perceval, tr. Dell Skeels. Seattle: University of Washington Press, 1966.

The Torah: A Modern Commentary, commentary by W. Gunther Plaut. New York: Union of American Hebrew Congregations, 1974.

Thoreau, Henry David. *Walden and Other Writings*. Toronto: Bantam, 1982.

Tillich, Paul. *The Shaking of the Foundations*. New York: Charles Scribner's Sons, 1948.

Todorov, Tzvetan. *A French Tragedy: Scenes of Civil War, Summer 1944*, tr. Mary Byrd Kelly. Hanover: University Press of New England, 1996.

Von Allman, J-J., ed. *Vocabulary of the Bible*. London: Lutterworth Press, 1958.

Von Rad, Gerhard. *The Message of the Prophets*. London: SCM Press, 1965.

Wiebe, Rudy. *A Discovery of Strangers*. New York: Quality Paperback Book Club, 1994.

Wiesel, Elie. *The Gates of the Forest*. New York: Avon Books, 1966.

——. *Tous les fleuves vont à la mer*. Paris: Éditions du Seuil, 1994.

Williams, H.A. *The True Wilderness*. London: Constable, 1965.

Yeats, W.B. *Collected Poems*. London: Macmillan & Co., 1965.

Young, Alexander. *Chronicles of the First Planters of the Colony of Massachusetts Bay, from 1623 to 1636*. Boston: Charles C. Little and James Brown, 1846.

ALSO AVAILABLE FROM NOVALIS

WALKING TO THE SAINTS
A Little Pilgrimage in France

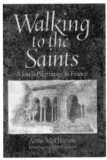

Anne McPherson
Drawings by Tony Urquhart

> "From the time I was five years old I knew France to be an enchanting country, a place of dreams…"

For Anne McPherson, this impression became more and more entrenched with the passing years. In *Walking to the Saints*, she visits time-honoured sites along France's medieval pilgrimage routes to Santiago de Compostela, reflecting on the architecture, the spiritual universe of medieval people, and the connections and contradictions between earlier theology and contemporary feminist thought. At the same time she discovers that each site, with its sainted patron and antique heroes, mirrors part of her own life's journey. With intelligence, freshess and wit, Anne McPherson invites readers to join her in walking to the saints.

The text is complemented by original, evocative drawings by well-known Canadian artist Tony Urquhart.

Praise for Walking to the Saints

"The chronicle of a lifelong journey of spiritual discovery is told with reverence, reality and humour. As Anne McPherson follows the wanderings of medieval pilgrims, her vivid responses to ancient French churches and abbeys echoed my own feelings of wonder at the sheer weight of time one feels in France. This book is a welcome invitation to explore the sense of eternity expressed by these hallowed buildings, and to join in the author's contemplation of what it is to be divine or human, Christian or pagan, male or female, ancient or modern.

"I was reminded, in the comments on the nomadic nature of the pilgrims, that the word 'saunter' comes from *'sainte terre'* (holy land) – a thought very much in keeping with the unhurried rambles that can be taken through this excellent book."—*Timothy Findley*

"A deeply personal account of a love affair with France and her romanesque churches, written by a born pilgrim (this is a woman who knows what is important), out of extensive life-experience. Anne McPherson travels restlessly, indomitably, with openness and honesty; she interrogates everything she finds. The reader will find it well worth hearing what she comes back to tell us."—*Margaret Visser*

Anne McPherson is a freelance writer and art curator. With degrees in English Language and Literature and Religious Sciences, she taught English and Religion in Literature at the university level for 14 years. She lives in St. Catharines, Ontario, and Campagnac, France.

To order, contact
NOVALIS
1-877-702-7773
or
www.novalis.ca

SPIRIT BOOK WORD
An Inquiry into Literature and Spirituality

J.S. Porter

> I have a story to tell—a story of my relationship with ten words and the writers who bring them to flesh....

LOVE: Raymond Carver
SMALL: Kristjana Gunnars
REVELATION: Flannery O'Connor
QUICK: D.H. Lawrence
STRANGE: Clarice Lispector
ZERO: Emily Dickinson
BEING: Martin Heidegger
TREMENDUM: Dennis Lee
OBEDIENCE: George Grant
MERCY: Thomas Merton

"J.S. Porter's account of his spiritual odyssey over a lifetime of reading reminds us, in his own brilliant phrasing, that we are wordmade creatures and that our revelations come to us by way of language. This is a book which makes the precious word fresh and strange, a book to visit and revisit for its insights, a book to read and dream on."—*Robert Adams*, author of *A Love of Reading: Reviews of Contemporary Fiction*

"J.S. Porter is our most generous, elegant essayist. He is also one of our very best critics. Wisdom, perception, humour, wide-reading, passion, quirky intelligence, a love of style – he has it all."—*B.W. Powe, author of* The Solitary Outlaw and Outage

"J.S. Porter is a writer who, in Rilke's phrase, 'grasps and truly holds' the work of others; and whose own work illuminates brightly."—*Linda Spalding, editor of* Brick *and author of* The Paper Wife

Born in Belfast and educated in Canada, J.S. Porter is a passionate and omnivorous reader. An accomplished poet, critic and teacher, his poems, articles, reviews and essays have appeared in *Grail, The Antigonish Reivew, Quarry, Brick, The Hamilton Spectator, The Ottawa Citizen, The National Post* and *The Globe and Mail.* He currently teaches literature at Mohawk College in Hamilton.

To order, contact
NOVALIS
1-877-702-7773
or
www.novalis.ca

AGMV Marquis

MEMBRE DE SCABRINI MEDIA

Québec, Canada
2003